THE UNFINISHED CHURCH

GOD'S BROKEN AND REDEEMED WORK-IN-PROGRESS

ROB BENTZ

CROSSWAY

WHEATON, ILLINOIS

ISBN: 978-1-4335-4006-6
PDF ISBN: 978-1-4335-4007-3
Mobipocket ISBN: 978-1-4335-4008-0
ePub ISBN: 978-1-4335-4009-7

Library of Congress Cataloging-in-Publication Data
Bentz, Rob, 1969–
    The unfinished church : God's broken and redeemed
work-in-progress / Rob Bentz.
        pages cm
    Includes bibliographical references and index.
    ISBN 978-1-4335-4006-6 (tp)
    1. Church. I. Title.
BV600.3.B465   2014
262—dc23   2013034665

Crossway is a publishing ministry of Good News Publishers.

VP		24	23	22	21	20	19	18	17	16	15	14
15	14	13	12	11	10	9	8	7	6	5	4	3	2	1

book. Here you'll find relevant questions, tough answers, and, perhaps most importantly, a pathway to life-affirming conversation about the stuff that really matters."

Dan Merchant, author/filmmaker, *Lord, Save Us from Your Followers*

"Rich with wisdom and insight, *The Unfinished Church* is for every believer desiring an enhanced understanding of the call of Jesus regarding the local church. In this transformational book, Rob Bentz takes us on a historical, practical, and enjoyable journey from an unfinished church on the pink sands of Bermuda to the gray corners of a garage in Michigan. Authentic, honest, forgiving, and humble, Rob writes with a deep understanding of gospel grace and the sovereignty of God while standing on the shoulders of giants like Bonhoeffer and Bunyan. *The Unfinished Church* paints a beautiful picture of God's long-term plan for the body of believers living counterculturally in a world gone mad!"

Jimmy Dodd, President, PastorServe

"*The Unfinished Church* is a refreshing reminder that God uses our unity in Christ as well as our diversity to reach different people for his kingdom. Rob Bentz helpfully outlines biblical truths about God's church, his bride, that are sure to bring contemplation, conviction, and a change of heart for those of us willing to be challenged."

Leah O'Brien-Amico, three-time Olympic gold medalist, USA softball

"Rob Bentz has written a clear, responsible, and Scripture-soaked take on the way God interacts with us, and the way we interact with Christ's bride: the church. Rob's love for the church is evident on every page."

Ted Kluck, author, *Robert Griffin III: Athlete, Leader, Believer*; coauthor, *Why We Love the Church: In Praise of Institutions and Organized Religion*

"Reader beware! If you don't want to be inspired to love quirky, diverse, often unlovable, certainly sinful people—like those in your church—well, put this book down now. Rob Bentz seems to think this is precisely what God had in mind when he redeemed us and planted us in a local church. Personally, I'd rather be entertained in a church full of people like me who are easy to get along with. Bentz says otherwise. Of course, he's right, which is why this may be one of the most important books on the church you read this year."

Mark Galli, Editor, *Christianity Today*

"No one is fool enough to insult a man's wife and then expect that man's companionship. But this is the strange spectacle we witness today: men, women, children loudly denouncing or openly ridiculing the bride of Christ, his church, and thinking that Jesus is happy to hear it. Even a careless reading of Scripture reveals the fierce and tender heart Jesus has toward his bride, and his swift judgment on any who seek to hurt her. *The Unfinished Church* is a clarion call for Christians to be the church, to love the church, and to serve the church until, as the apostle Paul says, we all 'attain to the whole measure of the fullness of Christ.' Convicting, wise, and urgent."

Mark Buchanan, author, *Your Church Is Too Safe*

"If you love the church and are not sure why, you are going to love this book. I'm a cynical old preacher who can't stay away from the church. Now I know why and I'm a bit less cynical. What a wonderful book! It's a gift to the church."

Steve Brown, Host, *Key Life* radio program; author, *Three Free Sins: God Isn't Mad at You*

"Bentz is right. Church is a group of struggling sinners who must pursue one another in love as God's community! It is essential for us to embrace this calling with joy if we are to declare the glory of the Lord to all peoples. There is no greener-grass assembly or ideal congregation; each assembly and every church member is in need of greater grace, patience, mercy, humility, and endurance from the Spirit of God. The church for whom our Savior died has a splendor that works in the midst of messiness. *The Unfinished Church* is a great exhortation to live out the gospel as people being conformed to the image of Christ."

Eric C. Redmond, Bible Professor in Residence,
New Canaan Baptist Church

"In a day when so many Christians doubt the importance of the church, *The Unfinished Church* is a richly biblical and practical display of what God is doing through his church. The presentation is popular, but not superficial. It is fun to read, but serious business. Every follower of Jesus needs to know what is in this book."

Richard L. Pratt Jr., President, Third Millennium
Ministries

"Here is a deep yet accessible book that paints a vivid doctrine of the church. Bentz's wide interaction with theologians and pastoral insights will benefit all readers. Excellent discussion material at the end of each chapter makes it 'small group friendly,' and his warm and hopeful responses may soften hardened critics of the bride of Christ. I highly recommend *The Unfinished Church*."

Chris Brauns, Pastor, The Red Brick Church, Stillman Valley, Illinois; author, *Unpacking Forgiveness*, *Bound Together*, and *When the Word Leads Your Pastoral Search*

"If you truly care about the struggle of integrating your faith into this modern world, please read *The Unfinished Church*. In this engaging and accessible book, Rob Bentz has woven together rich personal anecdotes, insight from astute thinkers, careful examinations of our ancient Scriptures, and even snippets from contemporary music into a focused, substantive, and tremendously helpful

To Bonnie

My wife, best friend, encourager,
idea generator, editor, and fellow journeyer.
This book has your fingerprints all over it.
You make me, and everything I do, better.
I love you.

To Reid and Bethany

Your easy smiles, bold laughter,
and heartwarming hugs bring me immense joy.
I couldn't be more thankful for you,
or more proud of who you are.
May your love for God and his unfinished
church continue to grow.

Contents

Acknowledgments

This book is written because of the triune God—Father, Son, and Holy Spirit. It is only because of the grace that God has offered me through his Son, Jesus, that I have been called, redeemed, and made part of his unfinished church. And it is only through the work of the Spirit in my life that I have anything at all to write. So, above all else, I must acknowledge the amazing grace that God has shown to me. I'm humbled by it all.

I am deeply grateful for the people God has used both in my spiritual life and in the writing of this book:

A group of people I affectionately refer to as the Unfinished Team spent time reading each chapter, offering feedback and encouragement, and praying for me throughout the writing process. This book is far better because of the faithful involvement of Bonnie Bentz, Don Brown, Wade Brown, Brian Cawley, Gary Coy, Josh Ellis, Geoff Henderson, Jessie Raedel, and Brian Roland. Each one of them deeply loves God's unfinished church and desires that others love it deeply too.

It has been an honor and a privilege to work with an exceptional team of professionals at Crossway. I am especially grateful for Dave DeWit, Amy Kruis, Keane Fine, and Thom Notaro, who have all added their expertise to this project.

The words of encouragement, prayers, and regular inquiries of my fellow pastors, colleagues, ministry partners, and friends at Woodmen Valley Chapel have spurred me on.

Vicki Ceass and the team at SonScape Retreats, the Straubs, and the Rolands offered me the tremendous gift of hospitality during my writing process. Thank you.

Two people were instrumental in this book even getting started: my agent and friend, Tim Beals of Credo Communications, who saw something in me, believed in me, and gave me the nudge I needed to take on my first book project; and my friend Cindy Limbrick of Awakening Artists, who often spoke words of life to me—from the moment that God gave me the image of the unfinished church as a book until the book was actually written. God used you both to make this work a reality.

Steve Brown and the faculty at Reformed Theological Seminary, Orlando, gave me a great biblical, theological, and practical foundation for life in ministry.

Our Bermuda friends the Johnsons, the Wests, the Groenings, and the Franks helped us figure out life on the island, experience Christ-centered community, and truly enjoy our stay.

My friend Dave Branon mentored me as a young writer for more than ten years. Your professional skill and personal wisdom have been a blessing.

Friends Dave, Rich, Paul, John, and Todd spoke words of truth to me in the early days of my faith journey. Thank you for your boldness and your consistency.

And lastly, I'm thankful for my parents, Reshard and Cheryl Bentz, who gave me a deep respect for the church and a foundation of faith. I love you.

Introduction

In the fall of 2000, my wife, Bonnie, and I moved from Michigan to Bermuda. We weren't exactly sure why God was calling us to this Nike-swoosh-shaped island in the middle of the Atlantic Ocean. But he was. God had woven together a strange tapestry of opportunities, unique circumstances, and relationships that simply could not have been arranged by human ingenuity. For the next fifteen months, we pursued God through his Word, through times of solitude and silence, and through the counsel of friends—striving to figure out just what his purpose might be for a young couple in such a remote location.

Once we unpacked our boxes, figured out the island's bus routes, and got accustomed to the sound of tree toads, we made a tiny cottage on Bermuda's South Shore our home. That's when we went to work pursuing God's direction for his newest islanders. We prayed. We engaged with a local church. We established relationships with other Christ followers. We served the Bermudian people in civic activities. We invested ourselves in the day-to-day lives of others. We asked God to use us any way he wanted.

And that's exactly what he did.

Our stay on the tiny island was nothing short of amazing! God did powerful things in us—stretching our faith, causing us to be more dependent upon him, and giving us the courage to reach out for help from the Christian community.

He also did his work through us. He used us to help others

truly experience Christ-centered community and to encourage others to engage in a deeper level of intimacy in worship. Yet our time was not all Bermuda shorts and pink-sand beaches. We experienced many relational challenges, more than a few personal doubts, and many fears. Quite simply, the months we called Bermuda our home were the best of times and the worst of times.

When we said our good-byes, gave our island friends our final hugs, wiped the tears from our eyes, and boarded the plane back to the States, we had a deep sense that God had changed us. And he used us to change others. Yet we were just beginning to get a glimpse of why God had plopped us in the middle of the Atlantic for nearly a year and a half. We hadn't built an orphanage. We hadn't planted a new church. We hadn't led hundreds of people to Christ. Yet a few specific images from Bermuda will forever be etched in our minds—the faces of friends, the beauty of God's creation, and a building. That's right, a building.

On the northeast tip of the island of Bermuda stands a massive nineteenth-century Gothic structure that is both beautiful and haunting. The walls stand tall and strong. But there is no ceiling. The columns are in place. But there are no windows. It's a ruin known to Bermudians as the Unfinished Church.

Construction on this historic landmark began in 1870, but parish infighting, financial difficulties, and a major tropical storm halted its progress.

Construction was never completed.

———————————

As long as we lived on the island of Bermuda, I was drawn to this structure. Its bizarre past. Its timeless strength. Its glaring weakness. Its imposing majesty. And its future.

One of Bermuda's most recognizable historical sites had a magnetic pull on me. I didn't know why. I enjoyed simply walking around the aging grey structure. I listened as the breeze whistled through its openness. I was drawn in by the unique angular shadows that were created by light pouring through places where there should be no light. I often took photos of the Unfinished Church under a bright Bermuda sun—or as a dark, foreboding cloud hovered above.

I loved to imagine what might have taken place within these walls had it ever been finished.

This structure caused me to consider questions that didn't seem to have easy answers. How could this have happened? Why was it never finished? What could God's people have done differently? What does it say about God's people? What does it say about God? This impressive though disturbing structure stirred something within me. Yet I couldn't quite put it into words.

Until now.

I've come to see that Bermuda's Unfinished Church serves as a brilliant metaphor for a similar building project that God is working on today—his church.

- His church is a beautiful historic structure *and* a vivid picture of brokenness.
- His church has a long and often sordid past.
- His church has shown great strength—in spite of its obvious and glaring weaknesses.
- His church is covered by the majesty of Christ.
- His church has a bright future, because Jesus is building his church!

To live within—and to love—God's church, requires an experience with God and his amazing grace. It also requires a solid biblical understanding of the church. It calls those within the church to make the intentional decision to forgive and love people who are often less than loveable. It demands faithfulness and commitment to God *and* to his people.

The Christian life isn't meant to be lived with a beat-up Gibson guitar tossed over your shoulder, and with a tattered leather-bound Bible in one hand and a Clif Bar in the other as you rest on a mountaintop somewhere in the Rockies. Christ's followers, made in God's image, are created for community with each other.

Rich, authentic, life-enriching, heart-shaping relationships are formed and nurtured within the community of faith—not outside of it. The encouragement and challenge for those who are disgruntled, frustrated, bewildered, or just plain ticked off at what's happening within God's church today is to stick around and do something about your frustration. Love God more deeply by loving his people more graciously.

Few things are as difficult! God's church is a gathering of broken people who do messy things. Yet the church is the beloved bride of our Lord Jesus. It's something that has captured his heart. While that's certainly enough of a reason to treat the church with heightened reverence, there are plenty of biblical exhortations to love Christ's followers with the same heartfelt passion that Jesus does. This alone makes God's church something we must not turn our collective backs on.

Bookstore shelves are filled with new titles telling the church what it ought to be and what it ought to be about: intentional discipleship, cultural engagement, missional living, and so on. Great ideas, but few address the biggest issue facing the church in our day—that few believers truly understand the significance of God's church, what God is doing in and through his people, and his long-term plan for the church.

That's a problem.

And even fewer believers actually live out the grace-centered love that we are encouraged to practice within this Christ-following community. Many of us tend to find the "one another" and "each other" passages, so prevalent throughout the New Testament, to be mere suggestions. They're things we might want to do, if it's convenient, for those we like to hang out with.

Our recollection of these passages changes, of course, when we are on the receiving end of a "one another"/"each other" exchange. That's when we often remember, with stunning clarity, the way Christ's followers are exhorted to live in community.

Bermuda's "Unfinished Church" (Lawrence Kent Photography)

Similar to the struggles that kept Bermuda's landmark unfinished, man's sin, cultural issues, and even the struggle to overcome natural disasters present challenges to God's building project. Yet one primary life-giving difference separates the man-made structure in Bermuda and the building project that God is working on—God promises that he will build his church.

God's church is unfinished. But he's working on it, and he's using you and me in the process.

———————————

As I write, more than a decade after we first moved to Bermuda, God continues to reveal his purposes for bringing us to the island. Some we've seen played out in our lives already. Some we may never know or fully understand. Yet none is more significant, more clear to me, than the imagery detailed on the pages of the book that you're about to journey through.

It is my prayer that you'll find truth, hope, and encouragement in these pages as you live in community with God *and* with his people—the unfinished church.

PART 1

THE FOUNDATION

1

God's Called-Out Community

But you are a chosen people, a royal priesthood, a holy nation, a people belonging to God, that you may declare the praises of him who called you out of darkness into his wonderful light.

1 Peter 2:9, NIV

When Christ calls a man, he bids him come and die.

Dietrich Bonhoeffer, *The Cost of Discipleship*

Each spring, the National Football League holds its draft of the best college football talent in the nation. Quarterbacks everyone knows and offensive lineman that only close family members recognize hear their names called by the league's commissioner. Every major sports media outlet captures these larger-than-life moments of the select few who have been chosen.

It's a big deal!

Thousands of talented college football players are eligible to be selected in the draft every year, yet only about 250 hear their names called. So, whether you are the first player selected and will soon be signing your name to a multimillion-dollar contract, or you're Mr. Irrelevant (the last player chosen in the draft) who'll have to kick and scratch and claw your way onto a team—you are significant. You've been called.

I've often wondered what it's like to be chosen in the NFL draft. What it's like to hear your name called as one of the most wanted, sought-after college football players in the country. What it's like to know that an entire city, state, and national fan base celebrates your arrival. What it's like to know that kids and adults alike will soon be wearing jerseys with your name sewn on the back. The magnitude of the experience and the fanfare that lies ahead must be exhilarating—and a bit overwhelming.

After a few moments of NFL dreaming, I realize that in a much more significant way—I am that guy! I have been chosen. I have been selected. I have been called to something new and exciting and much bigger than I can fully grasp.

You see, I have been drafted. I've been called out of darkness into God's wonderful light (1 Pet. 2:9–10). As a believer, I am now part of God's one-of-a-kind community of called-out men and women. I've been chosen, not by a professional football team, but rather by the God of creation. If you're a believer in Christ, you've been called too.

But this calling is different than any professional sports league draft. There are no team representatives for the Christian faith who'll quickly put a hat on your head fashioning an *ichthus* or a hip-looking Celtic cross. There are no reporters quick to ask how you feel about being called. And there's no large lump-sum signing bonus for the chosen. (Though, I've come to understand the eternal-benefits package is beyond imagination!)

Picture this; a holy, righteous God has called *you*. He has rescued *you* from darkness. God has given *you* his righteousness through the payment of his Son on the cross. He has freely given *you* his amazing grace. If these realities don't cause you to fall to your knees in humility, praising God, you simply don't understand.[1]

It's a really big deal!

Being called out by God, you have become part of a unique community of people called the church. This call is nothing short of amazing, but it does come with a few significant thoughts to consider, and a few challenges with which we must wrestle. First, we must consider the holier-than-thou issue. Then, we need to take seriously and embrace the weight of responsibility. And, last, we must acknowledge that we are a peculiar people.

Let's examine all three.

THE HOLIER-THAN-THOU ISSUE

So you're called out by God? You're one of his chosen people? You're part of a select club of holiness? Nice thoughts. Try wearing that badge of honor around when you start talking about your faith in Jesus with your nonbelieving friends. Curiously, these conversations tend to end rather abruptly because nobody wants to hear about how much God loves *you*. What your friends need to hear, see, feel, and experience is how much God loves *them*!

This, too, is a really big deal! (It's actually a huge part of why God called you, but we'll get to that in a moment.)

Humble recognition and acknowledgment of our called-outness is imperative when we interact with our nonbelieving friends. It's not that you and I were smarter than our friends and therefore saw something they couldn't. No. We didn't do the choosing, God did. This ought to bring us to our knees in gratitude and humility before our holy God. From this position of humility, we must submit everything about ourselves to him. We submit who we feel we should have been, who we truly are, and who we can ultimately become, because God's grace transcends our past failures and overcomes our current disappointments.

Once our heart's posture becomes one of humility, God can love us in ways that go far beyond our comprehension. He can—and will—pour out his amazing grace upon us. And this isn't just a midafternoon sprinkle—it's a downpour! God showers his people with grace. Once we've been drenched in this grace, once we've soaked in it awhile, then God begins to use us for his purposes.

The requirement is a heart of humility—a high view of God's amazing call on your life, and a low view of your role in that calling. He's made you a part of his one-of-a-kind community called the church for a purpose. This calling, this transition into God's community, serves as the foundation from which you worship God, genuinely love his people, and humbly serve others.

THE WEIGHT OF RESPONSIBILITY

As Peter the apostle wrote in his first epistle (1 Pet. 2:9–10), we are a chosen people, a royal priesthood, a holy nation called out to do something significant—to declare the praises of him who did the choosing. We have been chosen to declare the praises of the one who shined light into the darkest areas of our blackened souls and made us new.

How do we declare this? The answer is found in the powerful imagery of the text. The priesthood and our inclusion in God's holy nation are overflowing with Old Testament meaning and significance (Ex. 19:5–6).

Let's begin with the priesthood. Old Testament priests were a called group of men who had a unique, intimate relationship with God. A priest served as the mediator between God and man. Similarly, God's called-out ones—the royal priesthood—now have a special relationship with God and serve as mediators between the Father and nonbelievers.

Consider the weighty words of humanitarian Jean Vanier, who founded L'Arche community of faith for people with developmental disabilities. He writes, "The Church, like Jesus, is called to announce good news to the poor, liberation to prisoners and the oppressed, and sight to the blind. It is called to bring life and to help people grow to greater freedom and wholeness so that all may be one."[2]

Our calling, our being set apart, comes with a huge responsibility—and the tremendous privilege—of being God's priests to an unbelieving and dying world. As the Old Testament priest would offer sacrifices to God, so now the priesthood of believers offers the sacrifice of our very lives. We humbly offer our head, our heart, and our hands as a living sacrifice. We offer our head (our mind, really) as a sacrifice when we study God's Word, theology, and/or apologetic writings to be better equipped to answer the honest questions of our unbelieving friends. We offer our heart when we genuinely enter into the pain of a friend's marital struggle, parenting challenge, or financial difficulty. We offer our hands to whatever social issue is tearing at the fabric of our community—homelessness, underperforming schools, failed marriages, teen pregnancy, to name a few. We are called to enter into the greatest areas of need in our community.

Who needs you to be their priest?

> Christ followers are not promised financial wealth, physical health, a comfortable life, or any other self-serving reality.

WE ARE A PECULIAR PEOPLE

When Jesus calls you and me, we are invited to a life of sacrifice and service. It's a life of carrying our cross (Luke 14:27) every day with no illusion of earthly success—however "success" is defined in our culture this week (a huge bank account, a prestigious job, thousands of Facebook friends, etc.). Christ followers are not promised financial wealth, physical health, a comfortable life, or any other self-serving reality.

Jesus of Nazareth, the God-man we worship and serve, died in the most despised, humiliating, painful way known at the time—crucifixion! Why would we, Christ's followers, even for a moment believe that our day-to-day existence should be a life of luxury and pleasure? It's not.

This is why the words of Dietrich Bonhoeffer—a man who stood up for authentic biblical faith in the face of Nazi Germany and was ultimately martyred because of his stance—are quoted so often: "When Christ calls a man, he bids him come and die."[3] Christ followers who have an honest grasp of the day-to-day struggle to have one foot firmly in the twenty-first century *and* their eyes on eternity are those who genuinely live out Bonhoeffer's words.

Let's be honest; this is countercultural thinking. If you strive to live out your faith in this way, you're just plain weird when measured by the consumeristic, narcissistic way of the modern world. And yet, that's exactly why it makes sense for God's called-out community! He's called you and me into relationship for *his* glory—not ours. God has drawn you and me into a relationship with himself for *his* purposes—not ours. God invites you and me to a life of serving him, submitting to his agenda, and furthering his kingdom. It has little to do with us and our earthly desires. This isn't fatalistic thinking, either. Rather, it's an appropriate view of a holy God, and a healthy perspective of sinful men and women who are being brought to their knees by the amazing grace that God is showering upon them.

For the nonbeliever, this thinking—much less the entire way of life—makes little sense. Living sacrificially for the betterment of others is rare enough. Then consider that believers do so to follow the teachings of a man who died a brutal and barbaric death more than two thousand years ago. This is just too bizarre and counterintuitive for some of our friends to grasp—much less allow it to change the entire shape of their lives.

And if the personal sacrifice is not enough, let's not forget the most basic of all wants in our culture today—comfort and convenience. Participation with others in God's church really messes up a Sunday morning. Honestly, wouldn't it be easier to sleep in on Sunday, brew a strong pot of coffee, fry up some eggs and bacon, lounge around in your jammies, and get ready for NFL football? Of course it would. But we can't do that! God's called-out ones are compelled to something different. We're moved beyond our own comfort and convenience. We're drawn to something bigger. That's why it's entirely fair for nonbelievers to view us as peculiar people. We get up early, shave, shower, and do all the normal get-ready-for-work activities on our day off. Why? So we can meet with a group of other Christ followers to sing praises, engage with Bible-based teaching, and worship Jesus.

We *are* different.

God has called us, redeemed us (more on this in chapter 2), changed our hearts, and made us this way. He's pulled us out of a life of darkness and loneliness. He's given us a different view of the world around us. He's given us passion to praise him. He's given his chosen ones a different present reality—and a glorious future.

You're peculiar. I'm peculiar. Let's just go with it!

Old Testament Images of the Called-Out Community

Remember the NFL draft image at the beginning of this chapter? Here's where it breaks down just a bit: The players selected in the NFL draft have shown their value and worth before tens of thousands of screaming college football fans each autumn Saturday for the past four years. The highlight reel from their on-field exploits at a major university, combined with their raw athletic ability and their future potential, make them worthy of selection.

The people of God? Israel? Not so much. In fact, not at all. Consider Moses's words from Deuteronomy when he explains Israel's special place in God's heart:

> For you are a people holy to the Lord your God. The Lord your God has chosen you to be a people for his treasured possession, out of all the peoples who are on the face of the earth. It was not because you were more in number than any other people that the Lord set his love on you and chose you, for you were the fewest of all peoples, but it is because the Lord loves you and is keeping the oath that he swore to your fathers, that the Lord has brought you out with a mighty hand and redeemed you from the house of slavery, from the hand of Pharaoh king of Egypt. Know therefore that the Lord your God is God, the faithful God who keeps covenant and steadfast love with those who love him and keep his commandments, to a thousand generations. (Deut. 7:6–9)

On the plains of Moab, the people of God have been waiting and waiting and waiting to finally get to the Promised Land. They have been in exile for longer than you and I invest in raising our family or building our career. That's when Moses points the second generation of the exile to the facts—God has chosen the nation of Israel. He's chosen them not because they were special, significant, holy, righteous, wealthy, good-looking, or anything else. God chose them because he loved them. He chose them to show them he was faithful to the covenant that he had made with their forefathers—Abraham, Isaac, and Jacob.

God chose this group of people from slavery and tyranny

under Pharaoh because he wanted to reveal his character. He chose them to show his faithfulness. God chose them to reveal his amazing love. And he chose them for something even larger than they could imagine or comprehend!

One Old Testament scholar writes, "Israel was intended to model the character of God and thus be a witness to surrounding nations. . . . As 'priests' in a broad sense, they were to be mediators of the presence of God to the other nations."[4]

In the book of Exodus, Moses serves as the mouthpiece for God to his people. God's message to this group of people with nothing special on their collective résumé is clear and consistent: "Now therefore, if you will indeed obey my voice and keep my covenant, you shall be my treasured possession among all peoples, for all the earth is mine; and you shall be to me a kingdom of priests and a holy nation" (Ex. 19:5–6).

God chose a people with whom he desired a covenant relationship, a nation to whom he would freely give his special love and favor. What he asked for in return was faithfulness, devotion, and perhaps most significant of all—a willingness to be a blessing to others. God's people will be a kingdom of priests and a holy nation.

Bruce Waltke writes:

> God's election is not a blessing that can be enjoyed in seclusion by communities hiding out in the desert. It is not some private, individual assurance of material prosperity and physical health. It is, rather, a special status given to a people who by their divine calling must live before the eyes of the world, engage with the nations.[5]

God set his affection on Israel for a distinct purpose—that they would be a blessing to all nations. Throughout history, God's people have attempted (with varying degrees of success) to fulfill the high call of this awesome responsibility.

New Testament Images of the Called-Out Community

When you consider the language of being called out and chosen by God in the New Testament, the apostle Paul serves as the loudest and clearest voice. His letters offer strong images of God's grace showered upon a called-out community. Truth is, it's harder to find a letter where Paul *doesn't* use called-out language when speaking of God's people than to find one where he does. The apostle's writings to the different stops on his missionary journeys are filled with chosen, called-out language. Here's a sample:

> To all those in Rome who are loved by God and called to be saints . . . (Rom. 1:7)

> To the church of God that is in Corinth, to those sanctified in Christ Jesus, called to be saints . . . (1 Cor. 1:2)

> He chose us in him before the foundation of the world, that we should be holy and blameless before him. In love he predestined us for adoption as sons through Jesus Christ, according to the purpose of his will. (Eph. 1:4–5)

> For we know, brothers loved by God, that he has chosen you, because our gospel came to you not only in word, but also in power and in the Holy Spirit and with full conviction. (1 Thess. 1:4–5)

> We always pray for you, that our God may make you worthy of his calling and may fulfill every resolve for good and every work of faith by his power. (2 Thess. 1:11)

> Paul, a servant of God and an apostle of Jesus Christ, for the sake of the faith of God's elect . . . (Titus 1:1)

Paul begins the majority of his letters with a reminder, an acknowledgment of the believer's standing as one called, chosen, or elect of God. These reminders are there for a distinct purpose: to help believers connect with our true identity as called-out men and women. Paul wants us as God's people always to be mindful of who we really are. He reminds us that our rightful position before a holy God is humility—with privileges.

I often take the same approach with my young children. When I have words of encouragement or guidance, I begin with an acknowledgment of who they are as my son and my daughter—just to remind them that they hold a unique and special place in my heart. They have rights and privileges that no other children have. They are special—and specially loved. From this position of security, we can begin to talk and work through important instructions or actions.

Ultimately, being a called man or woman is a position of greatness. But it's obviously not of our own doing. Once Paul has established this fact with his reading audience—and only then—he presses on with the instruction and exhortation and doctrine that

> Paul's letters are typically addressed to Jews who have a heritage of faith. Peter writes to a bunch of Gentiles!

typically follow. It's our status, a "know who you are" idea, that drives Paul's subsequent call of God's people to God-honoring action.

The apostle Peter also uses similar chosen terminology in his first letter: "Peter, an apostle of Jesus Christ, To those who are elect exiles of the Dispersion in Pontus, Galatia, Cappadocia, Asia, and Bithynia, according to the foreknowledge of God the Father, in the sanctification of the Spirit, for obedience to Jesus Christ and for sprinkling with his blood" (1 Pet. 1:1–2).

Thematically, Peter's writing sounds very similar to that of the apostle Paul. However, these words are very different because they are written to a very different audience. Paul's letters are typically addressed to Jews who have a heritage of faith. Peter writes to a bunch of Gentiles! Peter is writing to "outsiders," yet he's using terms like "elect . . . of God the Father."

How can this be?

Edmund Clowney explains the significance of this often overlooked insight:

> Nothing is more astonishing than that he should call these Gentiles the *chosen of God the Father*. Israel was God's chosen people. . . . How could Gentiles be called God's chosen, his elect? . . .
>
> . . . These Christian Gentiles are God's chosen people because he has known them from all eternity. Jesus Christ was foreknown by the Father before the world was created. The chosen people of Christ are also foreknown by the Father. Their inclusion in the people of God is no accident, no afterthought, but God's purpose from the beginning.[6]

This opens up a keen point of interest and a door for major theological discussion. The Israelites, God's chosen people throughout the Old Testament, are not alone in God's ultimate plan of salvation and redemption. Peter introduces us to the reality that God's plan now includes outsiders—Gentiles. (This is a *really* good thing for those of us without Jewish heritage!)

Clowney continues, "God's choosing is the final reason that polluted Gentiles can be called his people. But God's choosing also means that he will act to make these Gentiles his own. To belong to God they must be redeemed from their sin and washed from its stain."[7]

Peter acknowledges the requirement of Christ's blood and the Spirit's work through the knowledge of God to bring about this dramatic change. Ultimately, Peter, the rock on whom Jesus would build his church, helps bring great clarity to the work of the Trinity in our salvation—our election as sons and daughters of God. Peter helps us grasp our place in God's called-out community, the church.

So What?

How does all of this talk of being called out, chosen, elect among the nations strike you? Are you humbled? Shocked? Confused? Do you now have more questions than answers?

I hope you sense a bit of all of these things. I know I do.

The fact that God would call out a special group of people to love, draw to himself, call his own, shower with unspeakable grace, and then entrust with special roles and responsibilities in his kingdom work is quite astonishing when you get to the heart of it.

But that's precisely where things often fall apart. This truth doesn't always get from the pages of Scripture up to our head and ultimately penetrate our heart.

Intellectually, we acknowledge the biblical facts. We nod in appreciation of these truths from the pages of Scripture. We might even worship with other believers in community, talk about our faith regularly, and enjoy some theologically driven intellectual stimulation. But that's where it often stops. We love the fact that God has chosen us and called us to himself. We gladly receive his gift of faith. We soak in the shower of his grace. With ease, we receive the benefits of his love and grace and forgiveness.

Sometimes, though, we take things a step further. We actually abuse the gifts God has given us by taking them for granted. But we're not alone. It's been happening for centuries. God's people have repeatedly underappreciated, overlooked, forgotten, and intentionally ignored God's special favor.

A cavalier, brazen attitude toward God and his kindness is nothing new. My son, Reid, often rolls his eyes in youthful sarcasm when we're in the middle of reading an Old Testament story from his children's Bible. He'll say, "Let me guess, Dad; God's people don't trust him. They turn to idols." The further we read on in the biblical story, my son is usually right.[8]

I often feel a bit strange and uncomfortable when we read of the unfaithfulness of God's people in the Old Testament, because I know that I'm often guilty of the same wandering heart. When it's my turn to respond to God in faithfulness, faithfulness is the very thing I lack. I tend to act like my Old Testament brethren more than I care to admit. Unfortunately, many twenty-first-century believers do the same. This fact is a bit odd, frankly, considering that we really have only one response to give—worship.

> Being chosen by God is based upon nothing we've done. So, this reality should bring us to our knees in worship. Does it?

As we've seen earlier in this chapter, being chosen by God is based upon nothing we've done. So, this reality should bring us to our knees in worship. Does it? If so, how often? I'm not talking about a guilt-ridden response. A duty-driven, dress-up, put-on-a-happy-face, go-through-the motions, politely-whisper-a-few-songs-and-prayers worship response.

That's no good.

I'm referring to a genuine heart posture of worship of the God who chose you and made you part of a special community. For some of us, this response may look like a raise-your-hands-in-the-air, dance-around-the-room kind of celebration. For others of us, it may be a matter of falling face-first on the floor, prostrate before the Lord, unable to speak. Worship with celebration. Worship with contemplation. Worship through singing, dancing, or speech. Whatever form it takes, you and I must worship!

John Stott, one of the most faithful churchmen of the last

century, acknowledged the importance of worship *and* another response: "The church is a people that have been both called out of the world to worship God and sent back into the world to witness and serve."[9]

These are our responsibilities as part of God's called-out community—the church. We've been called to live a life of worship and service (Luke 4:8). We've been called to offer ourselves as living sacrifices (Rom. 12:1). We've been called to serve as priests (1 Pet. 2:9).

As the church, you and I have been invited on an intimate journey with God. We are now challenged to invite others to join us on that journey.

I love the succinct way Christopher J. H. Wright describes the role of the church: "It is not so much the case that God has a mission for his church in the world, as that God has a church for his mission in the world. Mission was not made for the church; the church was made for mission—God's mission."[10]

How are you living out God's mission?

What area of your life are you sacrificing for God's work?

Are you expressing your priesthood?

What is your active response to God and his people? (Again, a guilt-driven response doesn't work.)

Our former pastor, Matt Heard, taught our congregation that worship is "our active, all-of-life response to the worth of who God is and what he does." I love this definition, because it captures the only worthy response that called-out men and women have to our almighty God—worship. Worship through singing. Worship through painting. Worship through writing. Worship through serving at the soup kitchen. Worship through your accounting practice. Worship through parenting. Worship.

As part of God's called-out, chosen, elect-among-all-nations community called the church, what is your priestly act of worship?

The Foundation

Church History

The truths discussed in this chapter have deep roots in the history of God's church. Consider the following example as you engage with these truths.

The French Confession of Faith, AD 1559

> XII. We believe that from this corruption and general condemnation in which all men are plunged, God, according to his eternal and immutable counsel, calleth those whom he hath chosen by his goodness and mercy alone in our Lord Jesus Christ, without consideration of their works, to display in them the riches of his mercy.[11]

Music

The themes discussed in this chapter have been expressed in both traditional and contemporary music. Below are a few titles to encourage you as you reflect on these themes.

> "Church of God, Beloved and Chosen," traditional hymn, by Frances Ridley Havergal
> "We Are the People of God," by Mark Tedder
> "What You've Called Me To," by Eoghan Heaslip

Questions for Discussion

These questions have been developed for you to consider personally, answer honestly, and discuss openly—engaging your head and your heart—as you process the truths of this chapter together in community.

1. Have you ever been chosen for something you didn't expect? A promotion? An award? Try to recall your deepest emotion in that moment. Were you humbled? Were you proud? Try to explain what you were feeling and thinking.

2. In spite of what many of us have been told, Christians are not promised financial wealth, physical health, or any other self-serving reality. Link this idea with the words Dietrich Bonhoeffer wrote a generation ago, "When Christ calls a man, he bids him come and die." What about you has died the longer you've been a follower of Christ? Explain with details.

3. When you consider the biblical truth of your status as a member of God's "royal priesthood," what comes to mind? What does this stir in your head and heart? Discuss.

4. What is your primary, active, all-of-life response of worship? How does this serve as your priestly responsibility? Explain.

2

God's Redeemed Community

For even the Son of Man came not to be served but to serve, and to give his life as a ransom for many.

Mark 10:45

You are not your own, for you were bought with a price. So glorify God in your body.

1 Corinthians 6:19–20

Our practical life is to be moulded by our belief in the Redemption, and our declared message will be in accordance with our belief.

Oswald Chambers, *Thy Great Redemption*

Silverware. A burlap bag full of the genuine stuff. That's what separates freedom and a return to prison labor for ex-convict Jean Valjean in Victor Hugo's classic *Les Misérables*.

The film adaptation from 1998 captures the power-packed scene. After more than nineteen years of hard labor, Jean is out on parole. He's got many miles to travel to meet his parole officer. On the journey, Jean knocks on the door of the local church—the home of the bishop. The bishop welcomes Jean in for a hot meal and a warm bed. Conversation at the dinner table is awkward at best. Jean, not well versed in table manners, gobbles up the soup as though he hasn't eaten in years.

Then, after everyone has turned in for the night, the bishop hears a rumbling in the dining area. He wanders down in his robe to find the silverware in a state of disarray. In the shadows of darkness, he turns to find Jean hiding behind a large cabinet. The two men's eyes meet. Then Jean floors the bishop with a powerful punch to the face. Quickly, he stuffs the silverware into his knapsack and runs off into the night.

In the morning, the local authorities bring a handcuffed Jean Valjean back to the church. They've caught the ex-convict with his knapsack full of expensive silverware.

That's when something amazing happens.

The bishop tells the authorities that he *gave* Jean Valjean the silverware. He then chastises a speechless Jean for failing to take also the silver candlesticks. "They're worth at least 2000 francs!"

The authorities are astonished!

Then, with conviction, the bishop pulls down the hood that hides much of Jean's face and speaks words of life: "And don't forget, don't ever forget, you've promised to become a new man. Jean Valjean, my brother, you no longer belong to evil. With this silver, I've ransomed you from fear and hatred. And now I give you back to God."

The bishop pays the price of his own silver to purchase freedom for Jean Valjean.

This is an act of redemption.

Redemption; it stirs our soul. It's the theme that makes us stand up and cheer at the movie theater. It brings hope where all hope seems lost. It's the story that causes us to watch a film a dozen times just so we can relive the powerful ending.

It grips our heart and won't let go. Redemption flips on the floodlights in places where darkness reigns.

For the Christ follower, redemption is not just *a* story—it's *our* story!

It's your story. It's my story.

Redemption is the reality of the price Jesus paid on the cross for you. His perfect life given as payment for your sin-stained existence. It's the only way that you and I could be released from the penalty that our sin deserves before a holy God.[1]

Jerry Bridges says, "Just as the diamonds on a jeweler's counter shine more brilliantly when set upon a dark velvet pad, so Christ's redemptive work shines more brilliantly when contrasted with our sin and the consequent curse that was upon us."[2]

- Redemption is what the believer has through the work of Jesus on the cross.
- Redemption, received by grace through faith in Jesus Christ, is your personal release from the bondage of sin.
- Redemption is your freedom.
- Redemption is your new beginning.

Getting an honest grasp of the redemption that Jesus has accomplished for his people is critical for a biblical understanding of the church.

Without a clear recognition of God's payment on behalf of his people, you and I will not see each other accurately. I won't see you as God's sees you—redeemed by the blood of his Son, Jesus. And you won't see me as God sees me. Instead, I'll see your scars of sin. You'll look at me and see someone tattooed from head to toe with the ink of sin, guilt, and shame.

We can't help ourselves. We don't choose to view each other this way. It's just incredibly difficult for one sinner to look past the sin of another to get a true glimpse of what God sees when he looks at his people. Instead, we see each other like the Unfinished Church[3] on the island of Bermuda—with flaws exposed.

This is why it's so critical for us to understand God's redemption of his people. If we don't, we will never see each other as God sees us—as redeemed men and women of a redeemed community called the church.

Do you see your brother or sister in the faith this way? You should. Jesus paid for them and for you. This changes everything! Your sin, and the subsequent scars that cover your body, have been, and are being, redeemed. This is how God views his people. This is why God's grace truly is amazing.

Because of the grace that is ours through faith in Jesus's sacrifice on the cross, the Father views you and me without all those bumps, bruises, and scars that sin leaves on each of us. Instead, the Father views us through blood-colored glasses of forgiveness.

> The Father views us through blood-colored glasses of forgiveness.

OLD TESTAMENT IMAGES OF REDEMPTION

Stories and images of God's redemptive acts weave their way throughout the Old Testament narrative. But it's not just imagery. Vocabulary specific to redemption is used about 130 times in the Old Testament.[4]

God's redemptive acts for his chosen people include the following: God's chosen people, the Israelites, have food when others do not (Genesis 46–47). They're spared God's wrath in judgment (Exodus 8–12). They're delivered from tyranny through miracles (Exodus 13–14). They have victory on the battlefield when the number of soldiers is shockingly *not* in their favor (Deuteronomy 7; 1 Samuel 17; 2 Samuel 5, 8). The ways God gives favor and performs redemptive acts for his people are nothing short of amazing!

Most Bible scholars agree the most significant act of redemption found in the Old Testament is the work of God in setting the captives free from the armies of Pharaoh in the account of the exodus.

Early in the story, long before God brings plagues down upon Pharaoh and the Egyptians, he reveals to Moses his redemptive plan. "I will deliver you from slavery to them, and I will redeem you with an outstretched arm and with great acts of judgment. . . . I will bring you into the land that I swore to give to Abraham, to Isaac, and to Jacob. I will give it to you for a possession. I am the LORD" (Ex. 6:6, 8).

But the Israelites, struggling to survive under the harsh punishment of the Egyptians, ignore the promise. They fail to grasp the promise of future redemption and deliverance. They totally miss it! The difficulty of their circumstances is just too large in their minds for them to have faith. "Moses spoke thus to the people of Israel, but they did not listen to Moses, because of their broken spirit and harsh slavery" (Ex. 6:9).

Isn't it curious how time moves on, generations pass, and we have the historical facts of God's faithfulness throughout the Old and New Testaments, and thousands of years of church history—yet God's people still overlook the current reality of our redemption. The thickheadedness of God's people is astounding!

Redemption seems far off, unrealistic, otherworldly. Like the Israelites under Pharaoh, we're often shortsighted. Like the Israelites, we often get stuck in the depths of our own messy circumstances and miss the future promise of God to his chosen people.

Only after experiencing the unfathomable—the parting of the Red Sea—did God's people awaken to the reality of God's faithful deliverance. Only after walking through a water tunnel of redemption did God's people respond in praise and trust for what God would do in their future.

Then Moses and the Israelites sang this song to the LORD:

> "I will sing to the LORD, for he has triumphed
>   gloriously;
>   the horse and his rider he has thrown into the sea.
> The LORD is my strength and my song,
>   and he has become my salvation;
> this is my God, and I will praise him,
>   my father's God, and I will exalt him.
> The LORD is a man of war;
>   the LORD is his name.

> "You have led in your steadfast love the people whom
>   you have redeemed;
>   you have guided them by your strength to your
>   holy abode." (Ex. 15:1–3, 13)

Yet even after witnessing a miracle so powerful and dramatic that it would make twenty-first-century filmmakers jealous, God's people continued their wandering ways. Their lives were marked by a cycle of sin, brokenness, and halfhearted repentance.

This embarrassing history causes us to ask, Why does God give special favor, complete with numerous redemptive acts, to a specific group of people? In God's sovereign plan, he will use his people to bless all peoples. Redemption comes with a responsibility to be a blessing to others. "I will make of you a great nation, and I will bless you and make your name great, so that you will be a blessing. I will bless those who bless you, and him who dishonors you I will curse, and in you all the families of earth shall be blessed" (Gen. 12:2–3).

Right there, in the text, all peoples on earth will be blessed through God's chosen, redeemed people. This truth isn't just for Old Testament scholars to discuss in the halls of academia. It's a truth that applies to God's people today. It's a biblical reality that should shape our theology and our practice.

This is why God's church, not some man-made governmental structure, must be the cultural leader in caring for the most basic human needs. This caring must begin within our own congregation, and it should reach into our community, be felt in our city, and ultimately touch those on the other side of the world.

At the church where I serve, we encourage God's people to bring a canned food item to church each weekend. This collection serves those in need within our body, and it helps supply the food banks in our city. But our call doesn't stop at our city limits. Like an increasing number of churches, we're also deeply involved in global initiatives to eradicate hunger and extreme poverty. This is not a model that we created. We didn't just have a committee meeting and decide that we'd toss a few dollars and man-hours at the problem. From the time of Moses, God has called his people to be a blessing to others. He's called us to pay the ransom for the freedom of others. He's called us to be agents of redemption.

> All peoples on earth will be blessed through God's chosen, redeemed people.

NEW TESTAMENT IMAGES OF REDEMPTION

In the New Testament, the snapshots we see of redemption are Christ-centered. The imagery is far more concise. Redemption is not about a rescue from a tyrannical earthly king, but about something much bigger, something eternal—the redemption of souls unto eternal life!

In Mark's Gospel, Jesus clarifies his mission to his disciples.

At the end of what had to be a disappointing interaction with James and John (amid their bickering and posturing about their ultimate and rightful place next to the Savior), Jesus says, "For even the Son of Man came not to be served but to serve, and to give his life as a ransom for many" (Mark 10:45).

Jesus's mission was intentional. He didn't come to start a religion, give people a name to spit out when they're angry, or become a cultural icon. Jesus came to pay a ransom that sin's cost required. Jesus entered humanity to pay the ultimate price, his own life, to redeem a people for himself.

The apostle Paul wrote frequently and with great clarity about Christ's redemptive work for sinful men and women. His letters to the Romans, the Corinthians, the Galatians, and the Colossians all show impassioned conviction that the facts of redemption must be grasped by Christ's followers. Then this grasp must lead to tangible action.

To the Romans

In Romans 3, Paul refutes a living-by-the-law gospel—which really isn't very good news anyway. Instead, he explains the gospel of righteousness through faith in Jesus, who made redemption available at the cross for all who would believe.

> Now we know that whatever the law says it speaks to those who are under the law, so that every mouth may be stopped, and the whole world may be held accountable to God. For by works of the law no human being will be justified in his sight, since through the law comes knowledge of sin.
>
> But now the righteousness of God has been manifested apart from the law, although the Law and the Prophets bear witness to it—the righteousness of God through faith in Jesus Christ for all who believe. For there is no distinction: for all have sinned and fall short of the glory of

> God, and are justified by his grace as a gift, through the
> redemption that is in Christ Jesus. (Rom. 3:19–24)

The impact of these words has reverberated throughout
church history. They inspired the Protestant Reformation as a
priest named Martin Luther grabbed ahold of the apostle Paul's
words "by faith" and wouldn't let go. Luther fought long,
experienced much pain and anguish, and was hunted like a
wild animal for his life-giving emphasis on "by faith" alone.
Luther stood firm. And this fresh view of the apostle Paul's
words literally changed the world forever!

John Stott notes, "The antithesis between grace and law,
mercy and merit, faith and works, God's salvation and self-
salvation, is absolute. No compromising mishmash is possible."[5]

This emphasis on righteousness through faith alone gives
people access to Christ's righteousness. It's not an unattainable
reality. Rather, "by faith" it is accessible.

Redemption also ripples through Paul's writing in Romans 6. The apostle rails against the sinful nature. He speaks
of its condemnation; its utter lack of freedom, its bondage, its
penalty of death. Then Paul explains the life-changing reality
of Christ's work on the cross in relation to our sinful nature.

> You have been set free from sin and have become slaves to
> righteousness.
> . . . But now that you have been set free from sin and
> have become slaves to God, the benefit you reap leads to
> holiness, and the result is eternal life. For the wages of sin
> is death, but the gift of God is eternal life in Christ Jesus
> our Lord. (Rom. 6:18, 22–23, NIV)

F. F. Bruce summarizes Paul's emphasis in Romans this way:

> Thanks to his [Jesus's] redemptive work, men may find
> themselves "in the clear" before God; Christ is set before

them in the gospel as the one who by his self-sacrifice and death has made full reparation for their sins. The benefits of the atonement thus procured may be appropriated by faith—and only by faith.[6]

To the Corinthians

Nothing in any of Paul's writings gives a more concise summary of his view of redemption than the words in his first letter to the church in Corinth: "You are not your own, for you were bought with a price. So glorify God in your body" (1 Cor. 6:19–20).

This is Paul's theology of redemption in bumper-sticker form. He gives us the facts followed by an exhortation. Paul wants readers to grasp the reality of their redemption. That's the indicative. Then he throws down the "so what" in the form of a challenge. That's the imperative.

Here's the breakdown:

- *Indicative:* Christ followers are redeemed. You are no longer a free agent. You were bought with the payment of Jesus's life.
- *Imperative:* Honor God in how you use your body.

Because redemption is your reality, Paul says: Do something about it! Honor God with your body. This is Paul's challenge to grab hold of the facts, let them penetrate your head (mind), soften your heart, and then put your hands in motion. Where there is a need in your church—serve. Where you find a need in your community—do something about it. Where there is a need on the other side of the world—go!

David Platt captures this idea in his book *Radical Together*. He writes, "We live sacrificially, not because we feel guilty, but because we have been loved greatly and now find satisfaction in sacrificial love for others."[7]

Once truth is established and understood, it must lead to action.

To the Galatians

One text that stands above all of Paul's other writings on the issue of redemption comes from his letter to the churches in Galatia. That's where he outlines the significance of God's redemptive work for his people throughout human history. In the third chapter, the apostle makes a strong point to link the faith of Abraham with the faith of those who now trust in Jesus. It's a powerful tie that binds God's redemptive act across time and Testaments.

> . . . just as Abraham "believed God, and it was counted to him as righteousness"?
> Know then that it is those of faith who are the sons of Abraham. And the Scripture, foreseeing that God would justify the Gentiles by faith, preached the gospel beforehand to Abraham, saying, "In you shall all the nations be blessed." So then, those who are of faith are blessed along with Abraham, the man of faith.
> . . . Now it is evident that no one is justified before God by the law, for "The righteous shall live by faith." But the law is not of faith, rather "The one who does them shall live by them." Christ redeemed us from the curse of the law by becoming a curse for us—for it is written, "Cursed is everyone who is hanged on a tree"—so that in Christ Jesus the blessing of Abraham might come to the Gentiles, so that we might receive the promised Spirit through faith. (Gal. 3:6–14)

The apostle states unashamedly that Abraham had saving faith. How can that be when Jesus hadn't even come to earth yet? Abraham had faith in the Messiah who *would come*—Jesus. It was a genuine faith. It was powerful faith. And it was a faith that set an example and a trajectory for all who would follow in Abraham's line—all who would be part of God's one-of-a kind redeemed community.

Later in the same chapter, Paul emphasizes the historical significance of Abraham's line of faith.

In Christ Jesus you are all sons of God, through faith. For as many of you as were baptized into Christ have put on Christ. There is neither Jew nor Greek, there is neither slave nor free, there is no male and female, for you are all one in Christ Jesus. And if you are Christ's, then you are Abraham's offspring, heirs according to promise. (Gal. 3:26–29)

Stott adds:

We have seen that in Christ we belong to God and to each other. In Christ we also belong to Abraham. We take our place in the noble historical succession of faith, whose outstanding representatives are listed in Hebrews 11. . . . we find our place in the unfolding purpose of God. We are the spiritual seed of our father Abraham, who lived and died 4,000 years ago, for in Christ we have become heirs of the promise which God made to him.[8]

As believers, men and women of faith, we have a lineage among the seed of Abraham—the children of God—that is breathtaking!

To the Colossians

Writing to the believers in Colosse, Paul deals with redemption in their present situation. He wants them to recognize that redemption is something they already have in their possession. Redemption has already been bestowed upon them by God. "He has delivered us from the domain of darkness and transferred us to the kingdom of his beloved Son, in whom we have redemption, the forgiveness of sins" (Col. 1:13–14).

This is true of Christ followers today, too. Redemption is

ours, right now. Do we have it fully? Of course not—we're unfinished. But what we now have only in part will one day be fully realized in glory!

A Story of Redemption

Just about everywhere a good story is told you'll find elements of redemption at its core. Likely, redemption is an undergirding theme in your favorite movie. It's probably the unnamed reason that you just can't put down the book you read at night before you turn out the light. It's probably one of the reasons you share your friend's soul-stirring Facebook post. Acts of redemption bring tears to our eyes, put a lump in our throat, and often cause us to make the daily choices in our lives with a bit more care and intentionality.

One example of this sort of care and intentionality comes from the small town where I grew up, Ludington, Michigan. Ludington is a beach town of about ten thousand people on the shores of Lake Michigan. It's best described as typical small-town America, where you actually grow up knowing your neighbors and the score of the high school basketball game.

A few years ago, a mid-thirties man named Jim began an intense battle for his life against a rare form of leukemia. Jim and his wife, April, who were both employed at one of the town's factories, spent their days traveling to a hospital nearly two hours away because the local hospital didn't offer the specific treatment he needed. Both time and travel became a burden for the young couple. It quickly chewed up all of their employer-allotted vacation days. As you can imagine, when one person is receiving invasive medical care and battling for his life, the other can't

> Redemption comes with a cost—but its impact is immeasurable.

afford to miss work and ultimately lose her source of income and health insurance.

The young couple was stuck.

Until their coworkers came up with an idea to help. Men and women from around the factory started to pool their vacation days. One worker gave three days, another four, and so it went. When the tally was complete, April received eighty-seven extra vacation days to care for her ailing husband.

Because their coworkers paid a ransom, Jim and April were able to enjoy months of freedom from the pressures and rigors of work to battle Jim's affliction together.

Redemption comes with a cost—but its impact is immeasurable.

Likely, you realized this cost when you first came to faith in Jesus. As you grasped the cost that Jesus paid for you on the cross, you were blown away! You were amazed at God's gift to you. Sadly, over time your amazement has probably waned. You're no longer as emotionally charged about your own redemption. Perhaps it has become an understood fact of your faith journey. Jesus paid the price, I received the benefit, and we all move on.

Sure, we're thankful. But if we're honest, it's easy to take our redemption for granted. The bumps and bruises, the scrapes and scars of everyday life, rob us of our ability to truly reflect on our own redemption. Ultimately, this robs us of our gratitude toward the giver of that redemption—God. I know this is true of my own faith journey.

I'm often reminded of this fact when I experience afresh the grace of our Lord Jesus as I participate in the Lord's Supper. The bread and the wine (or grape juice, depending on your denomination) of communion, are not magical elements. They're quite ordinary, frankly. But it's in this holy space, within the communion experience, that I'm drawn back to the cross anew. It beckons me to remember, once again, the ransom that Jesus paid to set me free. The smell, the texture, and the taste of the elements symbolize redemption.

These are also the moments when I'm most aware of the cost Jesus paid for my brothers and sisters in Christ as well. When I see a sanctuary full of believers genuinely entering into their story of redemption through their participation in communion, I'm often moved to tears.

Try it for yourself. The next time you experience the Lord's Supper, take a moment to look around you. Allow yourself to be reminded that the sacrifice of Jesus on the cross was for you—and for all of his people. It was a sacrifice for a chosen people who have been redeemed—and are being redeemed—for God's glory.

So What?

In our sin-stained world, situations of people in need of redemption are often right in front of us. Our kids play basketball with their kids at the YMCA. Our cube is next to their cube in the office. We send banal instant messages to them through Facebook.

Opportunities to offer acts of redemption pass us by like cars on the hectic morning commute. They present themselves in staff meetings. They enter into our casual conversations with friends after school and on the golf course. They are spelled out in front of us as we barbeque with neighbors. Why do we so rarely enter into these opportunities? Why do we shy away from getting involved in another's life? Why are we unwilling to be agents of God's grace and redemption?

I believe there are two primary answers to these questions. And both are a bit unsettling.

First, we struggle to believe in redemption ourselves. We know the depths of our "stuff." Wounds we've dealt others.

Promises we've struggled to keep. Goals we've never reached. We know too well, and too painfully, the brokenness in our own lives. These bruises and scars of our sin cause us to doubt our own redemption. Did Jesus really pay for *all* my sin? How can I truly be released from sin's captivity eternally, when I still struggle with sin week after week right now?

These are honest, real, authentic questions. Yet they are questions that actually have answers rooted in Scripture. And these answers offer a resounding "Yes, Christ's death on the cross paid for *all* your sins! You have been, and are being, redeemed."[9]

The payment Jesus made to set you free changes everything about you! It changes your history (your sins are forgiven), your present (you're free to live the grace-filled life God's called you to live), and your future (an eternity with him). As a believer, you have been redeemed and linked with a heritage that reaches back thousands of years. You are part of God's redeemed community—a people chosen by God, belonging to God, submitted to God's purposes. You are part of God's church. It's an unfinished, broken, and redeemed work-in-progress. But God is working on it.

The problem is that our doubt not only plays with our head, but also deadens our heart of compassion and our hands of service as well. If we're struggling to believe in our own redemption, how can we possibly offer redemption to someone else?

In the early 1900s, a young Scottish minister named Oswald Chambers spoke to a Bible college class and offered this challenge: "Our practical life is to be moulded by our belief in the Redemption, and our declared message will be in accordance with our belief."[10] We must truly believe in redemption. Genuinely experience it. Honestly express it. Then actively offer redemption to another because we believe!

The second reason is our unwillingness to pay the price for another's redemption. We ask ourselves, will the ransom of my time, inconvenience, emotions, and money be too much to pay? Sure, we might recognize a need, but far too often we choose to sidestep the cost. We make the easy move—and move on. Our self-centered response causes us to run away and hide. We do nothing.

This is wrong!

Instead, a genuine experience with our redemption should compel us to action. And this action should begin within the family of God. Because of this redemption we are willing to sacrifice for the deepest needs of others. The impact of God's redemption is different for those within the community of faith. It causes us to offer grace to those with whom we worship on Sunday. It causes us to offer forgiveness to those we gather with for prayer and Bible study on Wednesday evening. And it causes us to love and persevere with those we rub shoulders with at the local rescue mission on Saturday morning.

A healthy church, at its core, is a group of redeemed Christ followers—recognizing each other's place in God's unfinished church—living in authentic, honest, forgiving, grace-giving community.

Remember the bishop in *Les Misérables*? He bought Jean Valjean's freedom, and then he exhorted Jean to use that freedom for good. As a recipient of God's amazing redemption, are you living out the bishop's exhortation?

Church History

The truths discussed in this chapter have deep roots in the history of God's church. Consider the following example as you engage with these truths.

Heidelberg Catechism

86. We have been delivered from our misery by God's grace alone through Christ and not because we have earned it: Why then must we still do good?

To be sure, Christ has redeemed us by his blood. But we do good because Christ by his Spirit is also renewing us to be like himself, so that in all our living we may show that we are thankful to God for all he has done for us, and so that he may be praised through us. And we do good so that we may be assured of our faith by its fruits, and so that by our godly living our neighbors may be won over to Christ.[11]

Music

The themes discussed in this chapter have been expressed in both traditional and contemporary music. Below are a few titles to encourage you as you reflect on these themes.

"Your Redeeming Love," by Mark Altrogge
"I Have Been Redeemed," by Wendy O'Connell
"Children of God" (Third Day), by Justin Thomas Daly
"I Will Glory in My Redeemer," by Steve and Vikki Cook

Questions for Discussion

These questions have been developed for you to consider person-ally, answer honestly, and discuss openly—engaging your head and your heart—as you process the truths of this chapter together in community.

1. Have you ever truly considered the price Jesus paid for you? Whether it's the first time or the ten-thousandth time, take a few moments to contemplate the cross and Jesus's painful sacrifice that redeemed you. Discuss or journal an image or feeling that comes from your time of meditation.

2. Take another look at the biblical passages in this chapter that connect your lineage with that of Abraham. How do these passages influence your view of God? His plan? Your place in his story?

3. In Genesis 12:1–3, God's chosen people, the nation of Israel, were called to be a blessing to others. Since you are part of God's chosen people, how is he accomplishing his plan of redemption through you? Explain with examples.

4. Jesus also gave his life for the people sitting around you. How might that cause you to view them differently? How might it cause you to love or serve them differently? Explain.

PART 2

THE CONSTRUCTION

3

God's Eclectic, Intriguing, and Quirky Construction Crew

For the body does not consist of one member but of many. . . . But as it is, God arranged the members in the body, each one of them, as he chose. If all were a single member, where would the body be?

1 Corinthians 12:14, 18–19

The church is a diverse family of God's people, and in our diversity lies a natural and uncomfortable tension. We don't all get along and we don't all like each other. But we don't get to choose our families. They are chosen for us.

Rick McKinley, *A Kingdom Called Desire*

I'm weird. I actually enjoy going to the Department of Motor Vehicles. I find it intriguing to spend part of an afternoon at the DMV because it offers the best glimpse of diversity in our culture today. Skinny or stout, tall or short, married or single, successful or struggling, we all spend a day paying our dues at the DMV. Paying for the right to be part of the community of transportation.

The Department of Motor Vehicles gives us an accurate view of the people who make up our local culture. There are businessmen in dress slacks, hairdressers clothed in black, and homemakers looking casual with their kids in tow. There's the middle-aged woman who will slide into her Mercedes Benz adorned with a personalized plate, and the elderly man who struggles to find the flexibility to attach this year's tag to his Buick.

Diversity. That's why the DMV is such a great place to spend part of a day.[1]

It's different from hanging out at Panera Bread. Only a certain type of person is going to grab coffee and a cinnamon crunch bagel, enjoy some classical music, and respond to e-mails from a laptop at Panera.

It's not like spending time at the local Cabela's store. Only a specific segment of our population is going to be testing the weight and feel of the newest fiberglass fly-fishing rod. (Likely, this isn't the same person sitting in his second office—Panera.)

It's not like meandering around Bath & Body Works sniffing the soft fragrances of their body lotions and triple-wick candles. Folks who spend time and hard-earned money at Cabela's aren't typically concerned about eucalyptus spearmint hand lotion.

Sweet bagel, new fly rod, and aromatherapy lotion aside—everybody needs transportation. It's a commonality that unites us all. The DMV offers me a genuine glimpse of the broad spectrum of people in my local community. Folks I might not run into at Panera or Cabela's or Bath & Body.

But there is another reason I enjoy the Department of Motor Vehicles. Whenever I sit and wait for my number to be called, I'm reminded of another more significant picture of diversity. One with a global reach. A collection of individuals with a wide expanse of socioeconomic, cultural, political, and theological differences. A group with more examples of uniqueness than even the DMV can attract. God's church!

By design God draws to himself teachers and artists, contractors and caregivers, to be part of the unique group of people he calls his church. He created it that way.

God calls the poor, the wounded, the opinionated, the nosey, the caring, the broken, the seemingly unlovable. He calls them his own. He welcomes all of us, with our quirks and our maladies, into his unique community of love and acceptance, of grace and truth.

> If it were up to us to choose, God's church would look a whole lot like you and a whole lot like me. The Church of the Mirror.

This community is far different from anything you or I could ever dream up! Not because we couldn't pull together a group of folks that would resemble the famous "Buy the World a Coke" television commercial from the 1970s.[2] With a little help from our Facebook friends, we could gather a group from across the globe. Problem is, we wouldn't. The power of diversity is lost on most of us.

You and I would likely pick a group that looked a whole lot like us. We'd choose people who wear the same Eddie Bauer jeans, Gap sweatshirts, and Clark's shoes that we do—folks who drive Honda SUVs, make the same schooling choice that we make,[3] and live in three-name subdivisions.

If it were up to us to choose, God's church would look a whole lot like you and a whole lot like me. The Church of the Mirror.

Fortunately, God in his great wisdom, didn't draw unto himself a collection of clean-cut-Christian look-alikes, dressed in white polo shirts and khaki pants. He didn't draft a fantasy faith team of the smartest, funniest, best looking, and most creative.

61

The church that Jesus is building is an eclectic, intriguing, quirky, diverse mess of humanity. That's God's way. (Which couldn't be more different than our personal view of the world—and the church.)

It's All about Me!

Simple fact: you were made in God's image. It's true. Here's the evidence in black and white:

> Then God said, "Let us make man in our image, after our likeness. . . ."
>
> > So God created man in his own image,
> >   in the image of God he created them;
> >   male and female he created them. (Gen. 1:26–27)

Because we were made in the image of God, bearing his likeness, we are *really* significant. We carry with us the image of the Creator and sustainer of the entire world! (Take a moment to ponder that.) It's an amazing and humbling truth wrapped up tight in a skin-covered package that is uniquely you and uniquely me.

How amazing are we? God himself smiled on his creation. "And God saw everything that he had made, and behold it was very good" (Gen. 1:31).

It was *very* good!

But now, the very good thing has a problem. Our significance often causes us to idolize the created instead of the Creator. We worship self instead of worshipping the Holy.

Here's how it works: instead of thankfully and joyfully being little images of the living God, we make big images of ourselves and consider God the little one. We don't say this, of course—that would be blasphemous. But what we practice is a world centered on *our* thoughts, *our* actions, and *our* dreams.

Don't believe it? Consider for a moment the way you and I typically determine the quality or value of a photograph. It's a great photo if *you* look good! Right? Not such a good shot if your eyes are shut or your smile reveals a front tooth with a piece of the broccoli you had at lunch.

Here's another one: Consider the appropriate driving speed on the highway. *You* set the curve. Everyone else needs to stop driving like your great-grandmother and get out of your way, or they're certifiable speed demons driving like NASCAR star Jimmy Johnson! Right?

We tend to be the barometer of all that is right and true and correct in the world.

Obviously, these are two seemingly insignificant ways we position ourselves as the ultimate authority in our day-to-day experience. What we're really doing is slowly developing a mind-set where we elevate our thoughts and actions above God's plan and his desires. Unfortunately, our experience with other Christ followers often puts them on the receiving end of our elevated view of self. And, typically, we don't even realize we're doing it.

Anne Lamott captures the essence of this thinking when she writes of some honest counsel she once received: "You can safely assume that you've created God in your own image when it turns out that God hates all the same people you do."[4]

Can't see this sort of thinking in your own life? Consider how easily the mind-set takes over after a weekend worship service or a midweek small-group gathering.

- Are you critical of the music style of worship unless it matches the tunes in your iPod?
- Are you disappointed in the pastor's sermon unless it's filled with enough funny stories and memorable illustrations that you can bluff your way through a dinner conversation about the message's application for your life?

- Do you disapprove of the newly appointed elders who were selected to lead your church because none of them are guys you play golf with each week?
- Are you unhappy with the new person who's been added to the teaching team of your Sunday school class because he's been influenced by the wrong theologians and Christian thinkers?
- Are you critical of the book you're studying in your weekly small group because it's challenging the way you and your spouse are parenting your two children?

Your dissatisfaction and angst might be warning signs that you've begun to attend a church made in your own image. Built on your opinions. Fashioned after your desires. You've made yourself the senior pastor of the Church of the Mirror.

Unfortunately, this happens in the hearts and minds of Christ followers every weekend. You do it. I'm guilty. It happens in churches of every denomination, of every size, in every city. The Church of the Mirror mind-set infiltrates congregations everywhere—without much opposition.

Church databases are filled with people who came from the church across town. Christ followers shuffle from one local body of believers to another. Why? Because something's always wrong—the worship style, the volume, the pastor, the elders, the lady who wears too much perfume, the guy who's got too many tattoos, the folks whose tongues are too loose in the lobby following the service—all are *very* important. The real problem? Other people who aren't like that person in the mirror.

That's why longtime pastor Eugene Peterson says:

> The people we encounter as brothers and sisters in faith are not always nice people. They do not stop being sinners the moment they begin believing in Christ. They don't suddenly metamorphose into brilliant conversationalists,

exciting companions and glowing inspirations. Some of them are cranky, some of them are dull and others (if the truth must be spoken) a drag. But at the same time our Lord tells us they are brothers and sisters in the faith. If God is my Father, then this is my family.[5]

As the pastor who oversees the small groups at my church, I see this I-want-to-pick-my-family thinking with regularity.

If some members classify themselves as "deep" biblically and theologically, they're typically only interested in connecting with a group of Christ followers of similar depth. And if they can't find others to discuss the nuances and differences in the Synoptic Gospels or kick around the theological similarities of John Calvin and Jonathan Edwards, they're looking for another group of believers where they can experience "deep" community.

While there is certainly something unique in our culture about folks who still value a deep biblical or theological discussion, this desire often makes me wonder; who will be left to guide the younger, less-mature believers if all the people with biblical and theological depth are off swimming in the deep end of the pool of Christian community?

Another example I see often is the common interest in being physically active. Active people often want to invest only in others who'll bike and hike, camp and fish, and exert their inner Bear Grylls on the weekends. Common activities aren't wrong. Doing life together in a small-group community that has similar interests can provide us with powerful experiences and lifelong memories. But this active group is typically a made-in-my-image community. It's too narrow. Too self-serving. Too me-focused. It pays little respect to the diversity of God's church.

Pastor John Ortberg wrote an entire book on the oddities and quirkiness of God's people. In it, he says, "The yearning to attach and connect, to love and be loved, is the fiercest longing of the soul. Our need for community with people and the God who made us is to the human spirit what food and air and water are to the human body. That need will not go away even in the face of all the weirdness."[6]

Most of us long for a church community that is rich in worship, teaching, and relationships. We yearn for a worshipping community that regularly leads us into the presence of the Father. We desire a teaching community that is rooted in Scripture and is theologically rich. And we long for a community of Christ followers who are honest about living out their faith in word and deed. Problem is, we too often want all of these communities created in our image.

Rick McKinley pastors the Imago Dei Community in Portland, Oregon. His church is a diverse collection of urban professionals, former drug addicts, and young middle-class families. His clarity on this diversity of God's people is refreshing: "Jesus created the community of the church to be a family that comes into being by a new birth in Jesus and the miracle of our union with him. Jesus didn't create a product for us to evaluate and decide if we like it or not."[7]

The diversity that we see among the unique community of people that God is building called his church is something that we should run toward—not away from. It should intrigue us to know people—at a deep, spiritual level—who are unlike the person we see in the mirror.

The security that we have as men and women of our heavenly Father should open doors of opportunity that nonbelievers can only dream of having. Is there a safer person from whom to learn about an opposing political view than a fellow believer? Could there be a less confrontational environment to discuss racial issues? Isn't a fellow Christ follower the best person to help you understand the economic challenges faced by the poor, or the weight of responsibility carried by the wealthy?

The community God is building is incredibly diverse. And every one of us is better because the rest of the community doesn't look just like us.

THE THREE-LETTER EQUALIZER

Sin. It's the one core doctrine of the Christian faith that is misunderstood, minimized, or simply ignored by most of God's people.

Sin is not a topic that will draw the masses to worship on Sunday. Teaching about sin won't put any pastor atop the religious podcast downloads on iTunes. And a sermon series on sin certainly won't cause the people in your church to rise up and call you blessed.

It's just not popular to talk about the three-letter word.

But sin should be at the core of every honest discussion about God's people. Sin is the great equalizer. It puts everyone—the powerful and the powerless, the educated and the uneducated, the wealthy and the poor—in the same predicament.

> Sin is the great equalizer. It puts everyone in the same predicament.

The apostle Paul explains our dire situation in his letter to the Romans: "Therefore, just as sin came into the world through one man, and death through sin, and so death spread to all men because all sinned . . ." (Rom. 5:12).

All sinned. How about those two words? Because of Adam's sinful choice in the garden (Genesis 3), we've all been stained, cursed, tainted, diseased. It's called the imputation of sin. Adam sinned, and it infected us all. We're all in need of a pardon.

As we looked at in chapter 2, God's people are redeemed—and are continually being redeemed. Not because we are better than anybody else; rather, because of Jesus's sacrificial death on the cross for his people. It's called the imputation of righteousness. Jesus, the righteous one, died for the unrighteous. In this amazing exchange, we get Christ's perfection in a trade for our sin. He takes on the punishment that was rightfully ours. We're washed clean. Forgiven!

The image we are given from Scripture—fall and redemption—is the single most powerful image to unite the people of God. "What connects believers is the reality that we were all messed-up people, broken before a holy God, yet rescued and given new life in Christ. What unites believers is deeper than anything that can divide," write pastors Matt Chandler, Josh Patterson, and Eric Geiger in their book *Creature of the Word*.[8]

They're right!

Sin—and the forgiveness of it—is the one thing that should cut across the patchwork of our diversity. It is the one thing that should shatter the Church of the Mirror. It is the one thing that should unite God's people (not divide us), and give us a genuine desire to be used by God for his purposes.

God's Purpose for This Mess

When the apostle Paul wrote to the church in Corinth, a city where he spent a great deal of time (Acts 18) helping to establish a firm foundation for the church and to strengthen its leaders, he sought to address some internal divisions.[9] Misunderstandings about the status of certain people groups were among the chief issues of the day.

It's into this situation that Paul writes:

> For just as the body is one and has many members, and all the members of the body, though many, are one body, so it is with Christ. . . .
>
> For the body does not consist of one member but of many. If the foot should say, "Because I am not a hand, I do not belong to the body," that would not make it any less a

part of the body. And if the ear should say, "Because I am not an eye, I do not belong to the body," that would not make it any less a part of the body. If the whole body were an eye, where would be the sense of hearing? If the whole body were an ear, where would be the sense of smell? But as it is, God arranged the members in the body, each one of them, as he chose. If all were a single member, where would the body be? As it is, there are many parts, yet one body. (1 Cor. 12:12, 14–20)

We need to understand why Paul's writing in this rather abstract manner, using the metaphor of the human body. His reasons are twofold.

First, Paul wants every Christ follower to know that we are part of something bigger than ourselves (vv. 12, 14). We are a part of the body of Christ. Think community.

Second, Paul wants believers to see that we are also individuals, who happen to be part of the larger body of Christ (vv. 15–20). You are a part of this body, and so is the guy who looks, thinks, and practices his faith differently than you. You are a unique, specialized part. Think individual.

It may not seem like a necessary distinction—but when it comes to worshipping and living and serving alongside someone who is so dramatically different from you, these distinctions take on greater meaning. And the entire body of Christ is better for it!

At the church where I serve, a congregation of six thousand people, we have many different types of ministry. Some are up-front roles like leading worship, preaching, or teaching. Others are behind-the-scenes positions like stewardship guides or biblical counselors who serve to help those within our congregation. And we also have a group of folks who are passionate about serving the community that exists beyond our walls. People who serve food through our mobile kitchen, others who give time to children as reading mentors at our city's community center, and those who sort and distribute canned goods as we partner with food pantries to serve our city.

All are serving Christ. Some are serving in highly visible roles. Others might only be seen by the people they're serving face-to-face. Some roles might seem more honorable or praiseworthy, but they're not! That's what Paul is so passionately striving to communicate to the church in Corinth.

To merge Paul's teaching into our twenty-first-century church context, we wouldn't want our worship leader teaching stewardship courses. It's probably not ideal to have our reading mentors doing biblical counseling. Each Christ follower is uniquely gifted and an irreplaceable part of Christ's body. Irreplaceable!

McKinley believes that the misunderstanding we have of our unique gifts is nothing less than tragic: "One of the tragedies among the people of God is that we often don't believe that we are a miracle. The God who spoke creation into being created you on purpose, with a unique personality and personhood, and he gifted you to make a mark on other people's lives for his glory."[10]

Do you believe this? Honestly? Do you see your role as a bell ringer for the Salvation Army at Christmas as meaningful in God's kingdom purpose? Is your position as a Sunday school teacher to elementary school children fulfilling God's plan?

Problems arise within any group of Christ followers when we think too highly—or not highly enough—of our unique roll in God's plan. Our desire to be recognized and acknowledged gets the best of us. We yearn to be appreciated. We long for the accolades.

This has been happening for a very long time.

In Luke's Gospel, we're given a glimpse into the prideful

heart that lies below the surface of service to the King. "A dispute also arose among them, as to which of them was to be regarded as the greatest" (Luke 22:24). Even those who walked alongside Jesus in the flesh struggled with their place in his ministry![11]

Jesus's heart had to be wounded by his friends' immaturity. Yet his response didn't convey shame; it simply reinforced a message that he had taught his entire earthly ministry— humility. "Let the greatest among you become as the youngest, and the leader as one who serves" (Luke 22:26).

My son, Reid, has taught me much about this type of humility. For the past four seasons, I have coached his YMCA basketball team of elementary school kids. Reid has never been the best shooter or rebounder on the team. (He does, however, set the best screen at the Y!) He doesn't lead our team in scoring. But he does work hard at practice—and he has fun. He isn't concerned about the perception of others or individual accolades. How do I know this? One time on our drive home after a game, Reid said, "Dad, I'm not going to play in the NBA. I just *love* being part of the team!"

One-upmanship is foreign to a heart filled with humility, a heart content to be a part of God's called-out, redeemed, diverse community called his church.

Genuine humility is what God can—and does—use to accomplish his purposes in our world today. Skills? Yes. Humility? Mandatory.

It's Who We Are

We're dentists and database managers, accountants and architects, plumbers and pastors and paralegals. We love classical music and alternative country. We enjoy strong coffee and sweet tea. We take long hikes in the mountains, and we can easily spend a quiet afternoon on the beach reading a good book. We think deeply about politics and parenting. We travel for pleasure, and for mission. We pray from hearts broken by our own failures and sin. We gather to worship and sing from the depths of our souls.

We're quirky, messy, and stained by sin.

We're different by design. Because the church that God is building is *his* church. "We have been joined together in the church by God's grand design for a purpose that is far greater than any of us could imagine or achieve alone," writes David Platt.[12]

God is using his people in the unique places where we live and work to build his church. He's using our gifts and abilities and our experiences and relationships to accomplish the task. Humbly, we get to be part of God's construction crew.

Some of us survey the land. Others move the soil. Some of us dig holes for the placement of the cornerstone. Others pour the foundation. Some of us hammer and nail. And still others do the finish work. None are more important than any other. None deserve more honor than another. Nobody's role has more significance.

The construction crew is an eclectic bunch who don't always work well together, but God's called you and me to go beyond ourselves. We are to love the unlovable as he loves them. We must speak truth into difficult situations. He's called us to love orphans and widows.[13] He's asking us to be faithful with the tools he's given each one of us to use in our corner of the construction work site.

Now, grab your hard hat. There's work to be done.

Church History

The truths discussed in this chapter have deep roots in the history of God's church. Consider the following example as you engage with these truths.

The Westminster Larger Catechism

26. How is original sin conveyed from our first parents unto their posterity?

Original sin is conveyed from our first parents unto their posterity by natural generation, so as all that proceed from them in that way are conceived and born in sin.[14]

30. Doth God leave all mankind to perish in the estate of sin and misery?

God doth not leave all men to perish in the estate of sin and misery, into which they fell by the breach of the first covenant, commonly called the Covenant of Works; but of his mere love and mercy delivereth his elect out of it, and bringeth them into an estate of salvation by the second covenant, commonly called the Covenant of Grace.[15]

33. How is the grace of God manifested in the second covenant?

The grace of God is manifested in the second covenant in that he freely provideth and offereth sinners a Mediator, and life and salvation by him; and requiring faith as the condition to interest them in him, promiseth and giveth his Holy Spirit to all his elect, to work in them that faith, with all other saving graces; and to enable them unto all holy obedience, as the evidence of the truth of their faith and thankfulness to God, and as the way which he hath appointed them to salvation.[16]

Music

The themes discussed in this chapter have been expressed in both traditional and contemporary music. Below are a few titles to encourage you as you reflect on these themes.

"Come, Ye Sinners, Poor and Wretched," traditional hymn,
   by Joseph Hart

"Jesus, Friend of Sinners" (Casting Crowns), by Mark Hall
   and Matthew West

"We Are the Broken," by Matthew West

"Second Chance," by Rend Collective Experiment

Questions for Discussion

These questions have been developed for you to consider person-
ally, answer honestly, and discuss openly—engaging your head
and your heart—as you process the truths of this chapter together
in community.

1. Do you worship at the Church of the Mirror? How is this true
or untrue of you? Explain.

2. Consider the diversity within God's church. How is this represented in your group of friends, your small group, your local
congregation? What might you do to broaden your group? List
three ways you could engage with others who are distinctly different from you.

3. Picture the faces of the people God has brought into your life—
at work, in your neighborhood, at the gym, or elsewhere. Consider a few ways you are being used of God to build his church.
Discuss.

4. What are your spiritual gifts? How are you actively putting
into practice (or seeking to do so) your talents at God's construction site? Explain.

4

Love One Another

It Really Is about Jesus

Beloved, let us love one another, for love is from God.

1 John 4:7

A new commandment I give to you, that you love one another: just as I have loved you, you also are to love one another. By this all people will know that you are my disciples, if you have love for one another.

John 13:34–35

Without love, the outward work is of no value; but whatever is done out of love, be it never so little, is wholly fruitful. For God regards the greatness of the love that prompts a man, rather that the greatness of the achievement.

Thomas à Kempis, *The Imitation of Christ*

When Jesus tells us to love our neighbors, he is not telling us to love them in a sense of responding to them with a cozy emotional feeling. . . . On the contrary, he is telling us to love our neighbors in the sense of being willing to work for their well-being even if it means sacrificing our own well-being.

Frederick Buechner, *Wishful Thinking*

Are you fluent in multiple languages? Can you see things with great wisdom, and deliver truth into difficult situations? Do you have faith that could make the front range of the Rocky Mountains crumble into a Kansas-esque landscape? Do you reverse tithe, giving 90 percent to God's kingdom work and keeping just 10 percent for your own personal needs? Do you regularly give plasma—or, perhaps, have you even donated an organ?

I know—strange questions. A rather eclectic list of personal qualities and/or experiences. Truth is, I suspect that most of us would be hard-pressed to put more than one of these items on our résumé.

Most of us Christ followers build our personal CV with more overtly religious activities. We serve as ushers and greeters at our weekend services. We join the worship team or sing in the choir. We help out at the local food pantry. We coach at the YMCA. We sponsor a child through Compassion International. The good that we do for God is tangible. Most often, our activities are visible to our family and friends. And if we are completely honest, we consider our God-honoring actions pretty significant—even impressive.

> Without love, seemingly good deeds become acts of faux kindness.

Are they?

All of the activities on both lists can be great things. All can genuinely serve people in need. All can bring honor to God. All can also be a gross exhibition of pride, self-service, and ego. One key ingredient separates our actions as either blessing or curse—love. If we lack a heart of love, all the kind, generous, warmhearted actions in the world are worthless in God's sight!

How do we know this? The apostle Paul explains it clearly

in his first letter to the church in Corinth. A church that has lost its way. A group of believers who have become deeply concerned about status. A group of Christ followers more interested in serving self than serving others. Paul writes:

> If I speak in the tongues of men and of angels, but have not love, I am a noisy gong. . . . And if I have prophetic powers, and understand all mysteries and all knowledge, and if I have all faith, so as to remove mountains, but have not love, I am nothing. If I give away all I have, and if I deliver up my body to be burned, but have not love, I gain nothing. (1 Cor. 13:1–3)

Love is a big deal to God. It's what turns innocuous activities into monumental achievements for his kingdom purposes. Without love, seemingly good deeds become ugly self-centered acts of faux kindness.

Love. If we don't have it, don't give it away, don't offer it up freely, and don't exhibit it in our daily lives, we're nothing.

Without love our actions are useless résumé fillers for the wrong job.

The Source of Love

Love is not something we can simply muster up from deep within ourselves. We can't wish it into existence. We don't manufacture it. We can't create it.

Love has a source. That source is Jesus—through our heavenly Father. Read the words of Christ from the Gospel of John: "As the Father has loved me, so have I loved you. Abide in my love" (John 15:9).

Jesus encourages the disciples to grasp the Father's love for them—expressed through his actions. Remember, he's just exhibited this love a couple chapters earlier (John 13:1–15) by humbling himself to the point of washing the dirty, calloused feet of his friends. With these words Jesus has challenged his friends to a head and heart acknowledgment of God's love for them. He's encouraged them to live in this love. To bathe in his love the way you and I might soak in the direct heat that comes streaming through a window on a cool autumn day. To be restfully obedient.

God's people have been loved—and we are being loved. The Father gives love to us through our relationship with Jesus. We allow this love to enter our mind and ultimately penetrate our heart. We receive it, trust in it, and rest in it. Only then can we give love away to another. This God-initiated love is the fountain from which we draw love. It is the only true source of love for us to give away.

This progression of love—from receiving God's love, to living in his love, to giving it away—is the journey that Henri Nouwen so vividly describes in his classic book *The Return of the Prodigal Son*. Nouwen left a highly respected position in the world of academia to serve the mentally handicapped at L'Arche Daybreak in Canada because of what God did through the powerful images represented in Rembrandt's masterful painting *Return of the Prodigal Son*.

"I stand with awe at the place where Rembrandt brought me," Nouwen explains as he closes out his book.

> He led me from the kneeling, disheveled young son to the standing, bent-over old father, from the place of being blessed to the place of blessing. As I look at my own aging hands, I know that they have been given to me to stretch out toward all who suffer, to rest upon the shoulders of all who come, and to offer the blessing that emerges from the immensity of God's love.[1]

If the love of God in Christ fails to puncture the hard shell around my battered, bruised, and wounded heart, I will never be able to offer genuine love to another. Honest, authentic, sacrificial love will never flow from me to another.

Never.

Jesus knew this would be our plight. That's why he addressed his disciples, our forefathers in the not-fully-understanding-love business, repeatedly in his final hours. Again and again and again Jesus gave the disciples direct counsel to love.

First is the exhortation to love him by living in faithfulness—by living the way that Jesus modeled in their presence. In John 15:10, Jesus says, "If you keep my commandments, you will abide in my love." Jesus teaches that love is not mere verbal affirmation, but a life of practicing love.

Next, in John 15:12–13, Jesus emphasizes the importance of loving others—using his humble, sacrificial love as a template. "This is my commandment, that you love one another as I have loved you. Greater love has no one than this, that someone lay down his life for his friends." There is no way the disciples could have understood the intensity of Christ's statement in that moment. No way to feel his grief. No way to enter into his heartache. No way to sense his deep anguish. Yet Jesus was well aware of his immediate future. He knew these were his final moments with his closest friends. That's why he was so intentional to communicate, repeatedly, the power of sacrificial love to his disciples.

Jesus closes the entire list of exhortations in the first half of John 15 with yet another reminder of the importance of love. In verse 17, he says, "These things I command you, so that you will love one another."

Jesus's closest friends—the disciples—are the recipients of his direct counsel on love. And these are the very men who would ultimately put this unique brand of love into motion. The result of their faithfulness to the Savior's teaching can be seen in action in the book of Acts. We see the church multiplying, growing, and loving well.

The disciples, after Jesus's death and resurrection, ultimately got the point of his earlier emphasis on love. As twentieth-century Christ followers, do we?

THE SACRIFICIAL REALITY OF LOVE

Love is hard. Not because we don't like the idea of love. Who doesn't? It's the *action* connected with love that trips us up. Why? Because love is not simply an emotional thing. The New Testament clearly reveals that love is sacrifice.

Don't miss that word—*sacrifice*. It's central to God's love for his people. It's at the very core of what Jesus did, and modeled to us on the cross. And it is what every Christ follower is called to put into practice.

- It began with the Father's love for his people when he gave his one and only Son (John 3:16; Rom. 8:32).
- It was never more visible or more brutal than Jesus sacrificing his perfect life as payment for our sin-stained existence (John 10:15–18; Rom. 5:8–9; Gal. 3:13).
- It's at the heart of what Christ followers are to be about, living as little images of Christ—giving up ourselves for others (John 15:13; Phil. 2:3).

Today, the very idea of self-sacrifice is countercultural. That's just not what people want to hear about when talking about love. People want to think about long hugs and passionate kisses. They envision rose petals and expensive gifts. Love means quality time and your full attention.

Love has been hijacked.

Pop music, reality television, and date movies have cast a shadowy image of love on our culture that is as shallow as a sidewalk puddle after a brief summer rain.

Love is not always warm and fuzzy. It doesn't always give you butterflies and make you skip across the room like you did when your first crush told you he or she loved you. Love comes with a cost. Love causes you to place your wants, desires, wishes, and comfort second—behind the wants, desires, wishes, and comfort of the one you're striving to love.

To offer another person genuine biblical love is almost always messy, time-consuming, and hard work. That's why it's far more rare to see love lived out and put into practice than we'd care to admit. We can say that we love someone—a friend, a neighbor, a coworker—but our actions often reveal something less than love.

For more than five years Dave has served in a leadership position at a well-known Christian ministry. Dave is a gifted, articulate, visionary leader who has had a lifelong struggle with a specific sin. He's wrestled with it. Carried its shame. And he's sought counsel for this struggle during different seasons of his faith journey. Recently, his sin came into the light at his workplace. It wasn't a public matter. It could have been dealt with in a way that involved fewer than a handful of people. Dave owned his sin. He did so quickly and with genuine repentance. He sought forgiveness. He asked for help.

But to offer genuine biblical (sacrificial) love would have been messy and time-consuming for senior leadership. They may have been forced to answer a few difficult questions. It may have cost the organization some money in professional counseling. They may have had to sacrifice a bit of their personal reputation to enter into a plan of restoration for their brother in Christ. Instead of loving Dave enough to engage with him in a battle against a besetting sin—they fired him.

Gone.

The end result—a Christian organization not only said good-bye to a highly capable and creative employee, but they also subtly created a work environment where others can sense a genuine lack of grace, forgiveness, and love. The cost was just too great.

Biblical love—this was not![2]

You've seen this story before. Fact is, you've probably lived it yourself one time or another. Likely your faith journey includes a personal wound at the hands of a close friend, a parent, a mentor, a pastor—someone who had the opportunity to love you, but didn't because the cost was too great.

Maybe the time commitment was just too much for them to handle. Or their personal reputation would have taken a hit as peers would have questioned their sacrificial actions. Perhaps the emotional investment in you and your struggle went beyond their capacity to love. Whatever the reason, another Christ follower chose not to love you as Christ himself has loved you—sacrificially. You still wear the scar. It's healed, but the mark is still there.

This is not the way it should be.

The Practice of Loving One Another

Jesus said numerous times in the Gospels that we should love one another. That fact alone should make it easy, right? God said it. We believe it. Let it be done.

Not so fast.

Loving other followers of Christ can be tough—even when we like them! (And tougher still if they're about as much fun as the annual visit to your tax preparer.)

Practicing biblical, sacrificial love is something that Christ followers often fail at miserably. More than any of us would care to admit. But sometimes, in big or small ways, we get it right. Sometimes the love of Christ flows through us to another, and we love incredibly well.

As I write this chapter, I just received a text from a member of our church's pastoral care team. She was called into a situation of a man from our congregation who had died unexpectedly. After arriving at the hospital, she sent me a short text that said far more than the six words on my smartphone screen actually read. She wrote, "Incredible small group! Love in action."

The small group of believers had met at the hospital to support the grieving widow and her family. They listened. They prayed. They helped with travel arrangements for out-of-town family members. They offered love through the ministry of their presence. They loved well.

The ministry of presence is one of the most overlooked and underrated expressions of love in the church today. Don't believe me? Ask anyone who's lost a loved one in the recent past. They'll have no trouble telling you about its significance.

I know this from experience. My dad passed away more than three years ago. I can still tell you the people who loved on my mom, on me, and on my wife and our young family with their support. I can't recall the specific condolences they offered, but I still remember the faces of the people who sacrificed their time to enter into

> The ministry of presence is one of the most overlooked and underrated expressions of love in the church today.

our pain. I still recall the time family and friends spent with me in long phone calls. I still remember the firm handshakes and caring hugs from those who came to Dad's visitation. I recall the smiles and the tears of those present at the memorial service. And I remember those who stayed after to talk for a while. These people gave my family a great gift—the ministry of their presence. It has not been forgotten.

But offering love through the ministry of presence isn't just for those shaken by death and grief. It's also for the people who are young, alive, active, engaged in healthy relationships, mature, serving, and striving to honor God. These people need the ministry of presence too.

Ask yourself a few quick questions: Who invested in you early in your faith journey? Who got up early to meet with you over a cup of bad coffee and plate of cheap pancakes? Who discipled you in the Scriptures and in the core doctrines of the Christian faith? Who asked you the tough questions and walked alongside you amid the dark seasons of your life? My guess is that you can answer every single one of these questions. You can also picture a face and the location of where you used to meet. (If you spend enough time reminiscing you just might be able to taste that coffee again, too.)

Why do these questions bring back such strong images? Because of the ministry of presence. Someone loving you sacrificially with the investment of his or her time is one powerful example of practicing love for one another.

Unfortunately, Christ followers often consider this type of love optional. It's something we're willing to do when it's convenient. It's something to practice with those we like, and with those with whom we share the same interests.

Too often we think of Jesus's words as something we should strive for—a nice Christian goal. Problem is, most of us don't get too beat-up about it when we fail. We don't take our own lack of love seriously enough. Our inability to love one another well should cause us to wince. It should drive us to our knees in repentance.

THE MINISTRY OF LOVING ONE ANOTHER

Love is the signature of the Christ follower. It's our crest. Our logo. Love is our mark in a world crying out to be loved and to see love in action. Love is the one primary thing that God gave us to represent him. That's why it's nothing short of a tragedy when we do it so poorly. Our lack of sacrificial love for one another grieves the heart of God!

In John's Gospel, Jesus speaks boldly and with great clarity to his disciples about the prominent place love has in his plan for the world: "A new commandment I give to you, that you love one another: just as I have loved you, you also are to love one another. By this all people will know that you are my disciples, if you have love for one another" (John 13:34–35).

Why is this so important? Because Jesus knew that a contentious watching world would test the validity and significance of his life and ministry by the love his followers showed for one another.

This sacrificial love for one another, modeled and commanded by Jesus, proved to be a root of a branch that would grow and spread and produce significant fruit in the first-century church. So countercultural in their love for one another—and for those in need—were first-century Christ followers that they became mocked in society for their goodness.

Tertullian, the second-century Christian theologian, wrote on behalf of God's people in his classic work *Apologeticum*. Amid scandalous claims against believers, Tertullian wrote, "But it is mainly the deeds of a love so noble that lead many to put a brand upon us. See, they say, how they love one another, for [they] themselves are animated by mutual hatred; how they are ready even to die for one another, for they themselves will sooner be put to death."[3]

> We make the most compelling argument for the validity of the gospel in our life when we serve someone with an act of sacrificial love.

Far too often we think that our finely tuned apologetic arguments will win the lost. We think strong theological truths will sway public opinion to our side. Those aren't necessarily poor ideas—they're just not the most effective approach. We make the most compelling argument for the validity of the gospel in our life when we serve someone with an act of sacrificial love.

This kind of love takes on a variety of expressions. Big, bold, grandiose acts—like an unexpected financial gift that brings the recipient to tears. Or small, seemingly insignificant acts—like pausing to pray with a friend in the midst of his or her pain, thus leaving an indelible imprint of love.

Gerald Sittser writes, "Surprisingly, the church's success in this endeavor depends on only one thing; not great wealth, political power, sophisticated technology, superior organization, great preaching, public rallies, big buildings or creative programs, but the mutual love shared within the community of faith."[4]

Love. It's the ultimate apologetic.

Problem is, simple, sacrificial love is misunderstood, overlooked, and too easily dismissed. As with the Jesus-plus-works thinking we often apply to our own salvation, we want to tack on all sorts of add-ons, bells and whistles, and complexities to our acts of love. Add a tract, lots of extra religious words, a Bible verse or two—and we've got it.

Yet none of those things are needed. Just love.

But it can't be that simple, right? No, it actually *is* that simple!

This is why Francis Chan is so direct in his book, *Crazy Love*. He writes, "God's definition of what matters is pretty straightforward. He measures our lives by how we love. . . . According to God, we are here to love. Not much else really matters."[5]

The simplicity of this truth became extremely personal for me this past summer. A group of men and women (ranging in ages from late teens to early sixties) from my church traveled to the impoverished nation of Haiti. Our team spent one week in Haiti visiting orphan villages and Compassion International ministry locations.[6] We also were able to meet the families and visit the homes of sponsored children.

We didn't build a church, a shelter, or anything structural while we were on the island. We didn't run a camp, drill a well for water, or provide anything of tangible significance. These things are good, but this was not our purpose. Instead, we invested in loving relationships with orphan kids. We laughed with them. We jumped rope together. We played Frisbee, catch, and Duck Duck Goose. We learned phrases of their native Creole language, and we taught them some English phrases. We held their hands and gave them long hugs. And we prayed for them—by name.

Our time spent in Haiti was about nothing more than love! We sacrificially gave of our vacation time, our money, and time with our families to love orphan children.

Explaining this to family and friends upon our return was difficult. "What did you build? What event did you organize?" These were common questions all of us were asked upon our return. Our answer? We simply loved on orphans. That's it. And that was enough.

Our Struggle to Love Well

Love. It's what a watching world expects to see from Christians. It's what nonbelievers think following Jesus is all about. Doesn't it seem as though most Christ followers fail to give the practice of love the same degree of importance? How is it that we miss Jesus's commands? Why do we so easily dismiss our Savior's urgent final-hours plea?

Our own sinfulness gets in the way.

Deep within our own heart, we struggle to comprehend the sacrificial love that God has shown to us in the person and work of his Son. We have an incredibly hard time allowing the biblical truth that the Father sent his only Child into our world to love us—without conditions—to penetrate our mind.

And then, if we grasp this truth intellectually, receiving this love into our heart and soul is perhaps an even larger barrier for us to overcome. Why? Because we understand the depths of our own failures and sin, the act of receiving God's sacrificial love becomes incredibly difficult.

We want to believe it. We yearn to receive it. But something holds us back.

This is why loving another person well is so difficult. We can become so focused on our own need to receive God's love that loving another person becomes a struggle.

Phil Ryken says that a deep engagement with the gospel is the beginning.

> We will never learn how to love by working it up from our own hearts but only by having more of Jesus in our lives. The Scripture says, *"We love because he first loved us"* (1 John 4:19). Since this is true, the only way for us to become more loving is to have more of the love of Jesus, as we meet him in the gospel.[7]

If we can earnestly grasp God's love for us, we may still struggle to overcome the wounds we carry from a lack of love we have received from other Christ followers. And then, if we're honest, there's our own baggage that we tote around from our own past difficulties to love. We know full well that we have loved our brothers and sisters in Christ so poorly in the past that the very idea of trying again seems daunting. It feels as though we are sitting down to take a test we know we're going to fail.

Any one or all of those issues may be true. The pain we've experienced and the pain we've doled out have wounded us and others to such a degree that we've almost given up on intentionally loving like Jesus loved.

David Benner gives an honest assessment of the challenge most Christ followers face.

> My first response to the limitations of my love is always the same—to try harder. I pray for love with more fervor. And I try to love with more diligence. But nothing seems to change. Then I recall that I have got it all backwards. God doesn't want me to try to become more loving. He wants me to absorb his love so that it flows out from me. . . . And slowly, almost imperceptibly, I begin to see others through God's eyes of love. I begin to experience God's love for others.[8]

Just like the correct answer to nearly every Sunday school question you had when you were eight years old, Jesus is the answer. Jesus is the source of our love. Jesus is the model of our love. And as we allow ourselves to be loved by Jesus, deeply and honestly, the Holy Spirit will empower us to love others—well!

Church History

The truths discussed in this chapter have deep roots in the history of God's church. Consider the following example as you engage with these truths.

In his day, Emperor Julian the Apostate (332–363) desired to put new life and energy into the traditional Roman (Hellenistic) religion. He found it increasingly difficult to accomplish this task, for one primary reason—the sacrificial love of Christ followers in his culture.

To combat this challenge, Julian wrote a letter to Arsacius, high priest of Galatia, to exhort the pagans to live more like the Christians.

Paganism has not yet reached the degree of prosperity that might be desired, owing to the conduct of its votaries. . . . But are we to rest satisfied with what has been already effected? Ought we not rather to consider that the progress of Atheism [Christianity] has been principally owing to the humanity evinced by Christians towards strangers, to the reverence they have manifested towards the dead, and to the delusive gravity which they have assumed in their life? It is requisite that each of us should be diligent in the discharge of duty: I do not refer to you alone, as that would not suffice, but to all the priests of Galatia.[9]

Music

The themes discussed in this chapter have been expressed in both traditional and contemporary music. Below are a few titles to encourage you as you reflect on these themes.

"Your Love," by Brandon Heath
"They'll Know We Are Christians by Our Love" (Jars of Clay), by Peter Scholtes
"People of God," by Michael Gungor, Israel Houghton, and Brad Waller
"The Proof of Your Love," by For King & Country

Questions for Discussion

These questions have been developed for you to consider personally, answer honestly, and discuss openly—engaging your head and your heart—as you process the truths of this chapter together in community.

1. Read 1 Corinthians 13. Then reread it, inserting your name instead of "love." How does this change the way you read this text? Describe your thoughts and your emotions.

2. Jesus's death on the cross gives us the ultimate example of sacrificial love. How have you experienced this kind of sacrificial love from other Christ followers? How have you given this type of love to another? Explain with examples.

3. Consider how you have experienced the ministry of presence on your faith journey. Discuss the impact.

4. What is your biggest struggle to love others well? Is it your own difficulty in receiving God's love? Or is it the wounds you received from other Christ followers' lack of love for you? Or perhaps your past failures in loving others well? Or is it something else? Explain.

5. Give 1 Corinthians 13 another read. This time, insert the name of Jesus in place of the word *love*. How does this differ from the last time you read the chapter with your name embedded into it? How does inserting the name of Jesus affect the way you live out this biblical exhortation? Explain.

5

Encourage One Another

Giving a Blast of Gospel-Centered Truth

Therefore encourage one another and build one another up.

1 Thessalonians 5:11

When saints do sleepy grow, let them come hither
And hear how these two pilgrims talk together:
Yea, let them learn of them, in any wise;
Thus to keep ope their drowsy slumbering eyes.
Saints' fellowship, if it be managed well,
Keeps them awake, and that in spite of hell.

John Bunyan, *The Pilgrim's Progress*

Christian is on a journey. The path is long, winding, and treacherous. Like most journeys, there are dangerous pitfalls and enticing temptations along the way. Evil, carefree, envious, and ignorant people regularly cross Christian's path. On the journey, he is brutally beaten, is mocked, and almost succumbs under the weight of intense trials.

But Christian's trek is not a solo endeavor. For much of the journey, he has a traveling companion, Hopeful.

Hopeful provides encouragement when Christian needs it the most. He offers strength during Christian's weakest moments. Hopeful delivers exhortations and comfort with equal measures of grace and truth. And Christian offers Hopeful many of these same gifts in return. In spite of the intense challenges they face throughout the journey, both men eventually get to their ultimate destination—the Celestial Gate.

This journey, so vividly described in John Bunyan's classic allegory *The Pilgrim's Progress*, is your faith journey. It's mine.

The joys. The tests. The trials. The missteps. The failures. The sadness. The anguish. They're all there along the path. Like Christian and Hopeful, we have the scars and stories to prove it.

However, there is one thing that might be dramatically different when you compare Christian's journey with your own—you may not have a Hopeful in your life. You may not have someone to encourage you, exhort you, counsel you, or comfort you along the way.

There are many reasons that Bunyan's seventeenth-century allegory has become a true literary classic. The simplicity of the story, the rich imagery, the biblical depth, and the honesty all help to make this book a timeless treasure. Yet, one aspect of Christian's journey from the City of Destruction to the Celestial Gate steals my attention. The image of Christian and Hopeful journeying together, spurring each other on. That's the greatest strength of *The Pilgrim's Progress*.

With great discernment, Bunyan understood the importance of encouragement on the journey of faith. The Puritan preacher knew the Christian faith should not be lived alone. The temptations are too powerful—the trials too painful. Without help, the journeyer will not reach the final destination.

So, with vivid description, Bunyan gives the world Christian—but not without Hopeful.[1]

ENCOURAGEMENT: WHY IS IT SUCH A BIG DEAL?

Put yourself directly in the center of Christian's journey. (Remember, this is your path as a believer too!) You know the journey will be long. You still feel the rough edges of the scars of your troubled past experiences. You wince at the pain that your faulty view of the world has already caused you. You foresee sticky situations that will arise and force you to make difficult decisions. And then, of course, you live with the consequences of those decisions. Some good choices, some, not so good. And you are well aware that the path ahead will include plenty of people—well-intended or otherwise—who will negatively impact the journey. Danger, doubt, and deceivers dot the landscape in front of you.

Do you have a Hopeful? Do you have someone in your life who will give you positive, biblical encouragement? Is there someone who has the courage to give you truthful counsel when you've veered off the path?

Genuine biblical encouragement is among the most frequently undervalued and over-assumed experiences of the Christ followers' journey. Few of us receive enough of it, and few of us regularly practice giving it away.

Why is this?

We know how encouragement makes us feel. Strengthened. Empowered. Ready to press on! Why don't Christ's followers engage more consistently in encouragement? Why do we tend to be so stingy with encouraging words and actions?

Encouragement can quickly bring a smile to our face and a tear of joy to our eye. It can humble us. It can touch something deep within our soul. It can turn our mind heavenward and cause us to praise God anew. That's the way encouragement works. It's a blast of gospel-centered truth into a mundane or murky situation.

The apostle Paul understood this deeply. That's why

encouragement was such an integral part of his church-building ministry. He understood its power because it was modeled to him early in his faith journey. Shortly after Paul's dramatic conversion on the road to Damascus, he experienced support and encouragement from someone who regularly and sacrificially practiced encouragement. Allow me to set the stage.

Once Paul[2] reached Damascus, this man who was well known as a staunch persecutor of Christians was welcomed warmly by the local believers. They received the new man of God and ministered to him.

However, the Christ followers back in Jerusalem would not accept this dramatic life-change so easily. They were skeptical.[3] That's where the encourager stepped in.

Joseph, whom the apostles called Barnabas (which means "son of encouragement"—Acts 4:36), made straight the path for Paul's entry into the good graces of the apostles in Jerusalem. We read about this in Luke's account in the book of Acts (9:27). Barnabas had heard of Paul's conversion. He trusted it. So he spoke bold words of God's work in Paul's life. Barnabas's well-earned reputation earned Paul immediate favor in the eyes of his skeptics.

Paul: The Encourager?

After benefitting from Barnabas's faithful reputation, someone known as a trusted leader and supreme encourager, Paul began his gospel ministry. Traveling throughout the province of Asia, Paul sought to build and strengthen God's church. (Believers throughout church history have become very familiar with the details of Paul's work through what we know as the Pauline Epistles.[4])

Paul's original encourager, Barnabas, would accompany him on a number of his early missionary journeys. No doubt,

Barnabas spoke words of encouragement to the passionate convert throughout their time together.[5]

Paul was a good student. He quickly learned the power of encouragement. His intentional desire to encourage others can easily be seen in the heartfelt words of his letters to the believers in the churches that he planted, established, and served. Paul's correspondence to these different churches was packed with God-centered encouragement to the leaders in the community—addressing their own unique challenges and victories.

To the believers in Rome, Paul wrote of his desire to be with his fellow believers for the purpose of mutual encouragement. "For I long to see you, that I may impart to you some spiritual gift to strengthen you—that is, that we may be mutually encouraged by each other's faith, both yours and mine" (Rom. 1:11–12).

To the saints in Ephesus, Paul closed his letter by explaining the reason he had sent fellow minister of the gospel Tychicus—to encourage their hearts! "I have sent him to you for this very purpose, that you know how we are, and that he may encourage your hearts" (Eph. 6:22).

For the same purpose, using the same words, Paul sent Tychicus to serve the faithful in Colossae (Col. 4:8).[6]

Paul's ministry to the believers in all the churches he established was one of consistent encouragement. Paul commended the believers for what they were doing well. He exhorted them to press on in faithfulness to Christ. And he offered counsel amid the challenges they were facing and those that he knew would come.

All three of Paul's actions listed above are linked— encouragement, exhortation, and counsel. They come from the same root word, the Greek verb *parakaleō*.[7] All three forms of encouragement can be used of God to move a Christ follower successfully along the path to maturity—as Hopeful did for Christian.

Sometimes our response must be an inspiring interchange. Other times, a strong word of truth is necessary. And still other times, a listening ear and a caring word of comfort are needed.

This is why Gerald Sittser believes there's great significance in Paul's multipurposed perspective on encouragement.

> If believers flag in zeal and lose heart, we exhort them. If they struggle with a problem and stumble in their walk with God, we build them up. If they face loss and disappointment, we comfort them. There are many ways to apply this command because there are many ways our spiritual engines get run down.[8]

Last evening at our church's worship service, I paused to ask one of our small-group leaders how she was doing. Struggling to offer me a friendly smile, this faithful follower of Jesus told me that she was "okay." (Which, by the way, I've found often means the polar opposite.) I smiled and told her that her answer wasn't very convincing. Fighting back some very raw emotions, she allowed me to enter into her painful situation—if ever so briefly. This woman, who is old enough to be my mother, shared with me about how genuinely sad she's become because of her husband's continuous struggle with serious health issues. She admitted that she just doesn't have much hope. She feels alone.

And then she did something that surprised me. She asked me for a hug. I was honored. So I gave her an embrace of encouragement—from one Christ follower to another. In that moment, she knew that her pastor cared. She thanked me, smiled, and went into the worship service to offer praise to her heavenly Father, who—through the simple embrace of another journeyer—reminded her that he cares for her even more deeply than she can imagine.

This brief interchange brought to mind something I once read about encouragement by Marva Dawn: "When others are hurting, the greatest grace we can bring is to comfort or encourage them right in the midst of whatever they are suffering. A person doesn't need empty words, but the freedom to crawl inside a hug and feel the embrace of God."[9]

> Encouragement is God-honoring, believer-strengthening, church-building communication. It is biblically based truth spoken into the life of another.

Encouragement Isn't about You!

Encouragement is more about God than it is about you.

It's not simply a kind word. It's just not a verbal nicety. It's not pride-building flattery. And it certainly shouldn't make someone blush.

Encouragement is God-honoring, believer-strengthening, church-building communication. It is biblically based truth spoken into the life of another.

There is no better example in Scripture of this multi-layered benefit of encouragement than in the book of Hebrews: "And let us consider how we may spur one another on toward love and good deeds. Let us not give up meeting together, as some are in the habit of doing, but let us encourage one another—and all the more as you see the Day approaching" (Heb. 10:24–25, niv).

The writer is communicating the significance of encouragement for the edification of the individual Christ follower and the empowering of others. As you spur on a fellow believer, you strengthen the church. As you strengthen the church, God's people are better equipped to serve others (inside and outside the church) through greater displays of love and practical works of service. Encouragement has impact beyond the life of the individual Christian. It's an impact that brings the focus upon the ultimate and rightful recipient—God himself.

Encouragement is a tool that chisels away imperfections in the clay that is your life and mine. It's the spoken word, the typed e-mail, the handwritten note[10] that is meant for the personal growth of the individual, but not for our ultimate glory. It's anything from a quick phrase to a forty-five-minute sermon that shapes one's character more closely into the image of Jesus.

Kevin DeYoung writes, "Encouraging is not spotlighting a person but underlining God's grace. It is not about commending nice people to make them feel good, but commending the work of the gospel in others to the glory of God."[11]

DeYoung's statement got me thinking: How often do I see God at work in a believer's life and encourage him or her about my observation? Am I even looking for it? Do I freely acknowledge this as the work of God, or am I too self-focused to see Jesus in my brother or sister in Christ?

Far too often, believers become critics rather than encouragers. We question people's motives. We judge their actions. We jump up and down pointing our finger of guilt as though we're back in second grade sitting across the table from the person we suspect stole our chocolate chip cookie.

Why are we so quick to find fault in another Christ follower when we are supposed to be finding God in our fellow journeyer? Why can't we find Jesus in the heart of another, instead of finding the heart of Jesus's accusers in ourselves?

Encouragement should not be this hard!

Truthfully it isn't. The sins of self (importance, worth, and protection), our tendency to grade others on a curve of our own making, and our own deep-seated inadequacies all tend to get in the way of our capacity to encourage another. They inhibit our willingness to shine a bright light on what the Spirit of God is doing in the life of another. Yet encouragement is of critical importance in the life of the giver—and the receiver.

This is why David Benner writes, "The most important thing I can do is help the other person be in contact with the gracious presence of Christ."[12]

Look afresh at the words of the apostle Paul in his first letter to the Thessalonian church. He closes an entire section on the teaching of Christ's second coming by challenging the believers to "encourage one another with these words" (1 Thess. 4:18).

Encouragement is gospel-centered. It gives biblically grounded confidence. Encouragement offers hope for the future.

What Pilgrims Are Part of Your Journey?

In *The Pilgrim's Progress*, Christian has an encourager, Hopeful, who plays a dramatic role in much of the final stages of his faith journey. But Hopeful is not the only encourager that Christian has along the path to the Celestial City. He also interacts with many other encouragers along the way, people who are instrumental in Christian's making progress on his faith journey.

A few specific encouragers stand above the others in Bunyan's classic.

First is a man named Evangelist. He not only introduces Christian to the Way, but also shows him the words of God when Christian is first tempted to veer off course. Evangelist speaks words of truth (and grace) to Christian: "Your sin is very great, for by it you have committed two evils: you have forsaken the way that is good and have taken forbidden paths. Yet the man at the gate will receive you, for he has goodwill for men."[13]

Consider your current location on your journey of faith. Do you have an Evangelist? Is there someone in your life to show you the words of God? A fellow journeyer who will speak biblically grounded truth into your journey? Like Bunyan's Christian, you need to hear the words of truth when you're tempted to believe the lies that attack you every day in every imaginable way. This sort of truth-infused encouragement is critical to your progress on the journey.

Then comes a man named Interpreter. He introduces Christian to the unseen things of the faith journey. Interpreter helps Christian see that ideas and situations along the journey of faith often are not what they appear at first glance. There are deeper meanings that need to be discovered. There are layers, complications, and complexities that must be considered and wisely evaluated. Interpreter says, "I will show you that which will be profitable to you."[14]

Do you have an Interpreter? Some wise soul who has been on the faith journey much longer than you have? Someone who has greater depth of understanding than you do? Perhaps this is your pastor, who brings greater clarity to the Scriptures. Perhaps it is a personal mentor, who sees the path more clearly than you. Perhaps this is a learned Sunday school teacher, or a shepherd-like small-group leader, who serves to shine light on your path. Listen to their counsel. Hear their words of wisdom. Follow their direction. Your faith journey will be better lit if you do.

Then comes a man named Faithful. He introduces Christian to the trials that come along the faith journey. Faithful is the fellow journeyer who walks alongside Christian through the trials and temptations that are typical of the journey. He's honest about his own pain and failures. He shares his stories of overcoming.

Do you have a Faithful? A fellow journeyer who is going

through the tough stuff of life in a fallen world? Someone who is honest about failures, temptations, and struggles? Someone who asks for your friendship, prayer, and support for the journey? Someone who's willing to listen and enter into your struggles, temptations, and failures? Perhaps this is the person you meet with for weekly truth telling and accountability. Perhaps these are the people you do life with in the context of a small-group community. This is where faith meets practice—daily, weekly, and monthly—until one day you look back and recognize that you've journeyed together faithfully for years.

Evangelist, Interpreter, and Faithful serve as important pilgrims on Christian's journey. Their modern counterparts should play a similar role on yours.

Who's Encouraging You?

The day was gorgeous. A bright midafternoon sunshine glistened off the teal-blue water in Bermuda's Hamilton Harbor. As always, there was a gentle breeze blowing off the water, making the midday heat comfortable. This is where I was to meet my friend Nick. Our meeting would likely be the final time the two of us would see each other, as Bonnie and I were moving back to the States in just a few hours.[15]

We had spent many hours with Nick and his wife, Karin, during our time in Bermuda. We had gotten to know each other as friends, and more important, as fellow Christ followers. We had worshipped together, prayed together, and sought God's leading in our lives together. It was from this Christ-centered relationship that Nick told me that he had something very important he wanted to talk with me about before I left the island.

So, on a park bench overlooking the serene harbor, Nick and I made small talk about my travel plans and about my poor planning to move back to my home in Michigan in the middle of winter. We also laughed about a few memorable experiences we had shared together on the island.

And then it happened.

Nick made the transition from friendly conversation to powerful words of impact. He began to share words that humbled me. Words of deep, biblically grounded encouragement. Words that stirred something deep inside of my soul. Words that would ultimately change the course of my life.

Nick began by asking if I had ever considered serving God's church in pastoral ministry. Before I could even begin to offer an answer, he challenged me to prayerfully consider this vocational shift. He then told me that during my time on the island, he and Karin had witnessed the qualities of a spiritual leader (1 Tim. 3:1–13) in me. They had seen me love people like Jesus had loved. They had seen my passion for God's church. They had witnessed my desire to serve God's people. And Nick spoke words of affirmation and exhortation into my life with great love and conviction.

I was stunned! A man I had grown to respect deeply was now encouraging me and leading me in a way that I had never been led or encouraged before.

God used Nick as Interpreter in my faith journey. To guide me. To invite me to enter into the work that God had already been doing in my own heart. To help bring clarity and a deeper understanding than what I could ever have envisioned on my own. Nick was my encourager, my exhorter, and my counselor.

Nick's words of encouragement spurred me on to a journey. A journey of seeking God's will and calling on my life. A journey deeper into God's Word. A journey of more open-handed times of prayer with the Father. A journey into seeking the counsel of other trusted, mature believers. A journey that would ultimately lead me to seminary and into the pastorate.

This sort of encouragement is rare. It shouldn't be.

Nick was simply being faithful to what the Holy Spirit was leading him to do. He was intentional to encourage me in a biblically grounded way. I was the recipient of bold, genuine, gospel-centered encouragement. My life is dramatically different because of it.

I realize that most Christ followers have not had a Nick in their life, someone whose encouragement dramatically changed the course of their faith journey. Perhaps, the encouragement you've received has been more subtle, less dramatic, and not as journey altering. Yet, if we pause to reflect on our faith journey, most of us can point to at least one experience with encouragement. There was someone who comforted us during a difficult time. There was a friend who counseled us in the midst of a critical decision. There was a mentor who spoke honestly when we needed a strong word of exhortation. We haven't thought about the role they played in our journey because encouragement was often overlooked, taken for granted, or undervalued.

> If you're not being encouraged, don't wait for it to happen. Welcome others to speak into your life.

It shouldn't be.

What can we do about this tremendous need in our life? Seek it out. Seriously. Invite close friends, mature believers, and people whose faith journey you admire to speak into your life. Give them the holy space to encourage you. Allow them the freedom to comfort or counsel you. Give them permission to challenge or exhort you. What your encourager says may not be what you *want* to hear, but it might just be what you *need* to hear.

If you're not being encouraged on your faith journey, don't wait for it to happen; do something about it. Welcome others to speak into your life.

WHO'S YOUR CHRISTIAN?

Throughout Bunyan's allegory, Christian needed truth spoken to him by his friend and encourager Hopeful. And, likewise, Hopeful needed the biblically grounded words of Christian. One gives encouragement while the other receives it, and vice versa. That's a healthy rhythm for the faith journey. Unfortunately, it's a rhythm that many of us don't have.

We've already considered who's encouraging us—a Hopeful, an Evangelist, an Interpreter, a Faithful, or someone else. Now the question must be turned around. Who's your Christian?

This is a question that strikes at the heart of something we actually have a great deal of control over. Who am I encouraging? Whose journey am I speaking into? In both intentional and casual ways, we can be used of God to deeply affect the faith journey of another when we make ourselves available to others.

Who doesn't want to be encouraged? Who doesn't desire, crave, or yearn for a fellow journeyer to speak words of genuine biblical encouragement? Seriously, do you know of anyone who wouldn't welcome gospel-centered encouragement?

This is why words of encouragement should flow freely. They should be among the first things we offer another journeyer. Something we strive to give. Something we seek out.

Why does it seem to be so difficult? Why does it so often seem that most of us have to grit our teeth, exhale, and then eventually squeak out a word or two of encouragement? Again, it shouldn't be this hard. Unless, of course, we're just not paying close enough attention to the actions of those we're journeying alongside. Could it be that we're not seeing Jesus displayed in the life of our brother or sister in faith because we're not looking for him?

Regularly, I must take the attention off of myself, off of my own struggles and personal victories, to be able to see what God is doing in and through the lives of my friends. I can't be so self-focused that God's work in those around me goes unnoticed. This sort of attention is not solely for the benefit of my friend's personal faith journey, either. It also serves to further the gospel. It serves the greater ministry of the church as it keeps people moving toward God, and it gives them fuel to keep following the Spirit's leading in their life. This is why Sittser refers to encouragement as "the maintenance ministry of the church."[16]

Encouragement is like a pleasant breeze on a hot summer day. It refreshes. It offers a moment of relief and joy. And it's something that can even cause you to thank God for his grace in the moment.

The most concise words I've encountered about the importance of encouragement come from Dietrich Bonhoeffer. He writes:

> The Christian needs another Christian who speaks God's Word to him. He needs him again and again when he becomes uncertain and discouraged. . . . He needs his brother solely because of Jesus Christ. The Christ in his own heart is weaker than the Christ in the word of his brother; his own heart is uncertain, his brother's is sure.[17]

Christ followers *need* encouragement. It's something we must passionately pursue for ourselves and intentionally seek to offer to others on the journey. The strength of the church depends on it.

Encouragement is gospel-centered, Christ-honoring, Spirit-led, church-building, individual-strengthening communication. Speak it. Write it. Type it. Preach it. Teach it. Be someone's Hopeful and offer encouragement freely.

Church History

The truths discussed in this chapter have deep roots in the history of God's church. Consider the following example as you engage with these truths.

Few individuals have shaped the history of Christianity as much as Reformer John Calvin. Many caricatures of the French theologian exist—rigid, opinionated, workaholic, scholar, and so on. All arguably have a shred of truth and some measure of exaggeration. One narrative that is rarely discussed in examinations of the life of Calvin is the role that a wise encourager named Martin Bucer played in Calvin's life.

Bucer, a former Dominican monk, had become a well-respected leader in the Protestant movement throughout Germany, Switzerland, and much of Europe. He had been in correspondence with the younger Calvin through letters across the miles. These letters were not always filled with friendly banter; rather they often consisted of a high degree of debate and theological discourse between the two Reformers. This honest, edgy, and sometimes contentious communication didn't stop Bucer from providing one of the most significant examples of encouragement in church history!

During a critical transition time in the life of Calvin, after he had been banished from both France and Geneva, Bucer invited Calvin to Strasbourg. The city offered a scholar like Calvin plenty of possibilities, but that wasn't what Bucer had in mind. Instead, he had a deep sense of the need for a pastor to serve the French refugee church in Strasbourg, and a strong conviction of Calvin's strong pastoral gifts. The fatherly Bucer encouraged Calvin (think exhortation and counsel) to make Strasbourg his home instead of continuing on to Basel as Calvin was planning.

Calvin listened. He responded in obedience to his encourager's challenge and stayed in Strasbourg. It was here that Calvin began to preach and to put into motion a local church as he had always envisioned—one that was closely regulated by Scripture.

One biographer summarizes the outcome of Calvin's decision to follow Bucer's encouragement and stay in Strasbourg this way: "It was in Strasbourg that Calvin was born. Not actually, of course, but it was his birthplace as a theologian and church leader. . . . And so it was in Strasbourg that virtually all the theological influences came together to form the Calvin—and the Calvinism—known today."[18]

Music

The themes discussed in this chapter have been expressed in both traditional and contemporary music. Below are a few titles to encourage you as you reflect on these themes.

"Shelter," by Jars of Clay
"We Need Each Other," by Sanctus Real
"Words," by Hawk Nelson

Questions for Discussion

These questions have been developed for you to consider personally, answer honestly, and discuss openly—engaging your head and your heart—as you process the truths of this chapter together in community.

1. The chapter begins by examining the mutual encouragement that Bunyan's character Christian experiences with his friend Hopeful, in the classic *The Pilgrim's Progress*. What are your thoughts about encouragement after reading this brief summary? Explain.

2. The chapter says, "Genuine biblical encouragement is among the most frequently undervalued and over-assumed experiences of the Christ followers' journey." Do you believe encouragement is undervalued and over-assumed? Why or why not?

3. Three words—*encouragement, exhortation,* and *counsel*—come from the same Greek root word *parakaleō*. Which expression have

you most frequently experienced on your faith journey? Discuss the impact.

4. Consider the distinction between encouragement and flattery. How might this change the way you seek to encourage others? Explain.

5. Do you find it harder to receive biblical encouragement (exhortation/counsel) or to offer it to other Christ followers? Explain.

6. How has this chapter shaped or reshaped your thinking about encouragement? Discuss.

6

Serve One Another

Putting Our Hands into Action—and More

For you were called to freedom, brothers. Only do not use your freedom as an opportunity for the flesh, but through love serve one another.

Galatians 5:13

This much is certain: if we are Christians we must spend our lives in the service of God and man.

John Stott, *Christian Mission in the Modern World*

Because of the gospel, we serve because our hearts are overwhelmed with gratitude. Because of the gospel, believers can serve in freedom and joy.

Matt Chandler, Josh Patterson, and Eric Geiger,
Creature of the Word

Dietrich Bonhoeffer. A simple reference to his name elicits respect. Bonhoeffer's mind was brilliant. His theological ideas were sharp. His zeal for biblical truth was unwavering. His passion for God and his church were unquestioned.

The story of Dietrich Bonhoeffer has been told, retold, and written about with great frequency, tremendous detail, and exceptional writing acumen in recent years. Numerous books have been written about his life and his theology. Documentaries have been made of his story of martyrdom. His death at the hands of the Nazis near the end of World War II is well known. Yet one thing that is often mentioned but rarely emphasized is perhaps the greatest of all of Bonhoeffer's desires—to sacrificially serve God by serving God's people. I believe this is Bonhoeffer's greatest legacy!

Here's the background: In 1939, churches throughout Germany were bowing a collective knee to Adolf Hitler. Pressure was mounting for churches and their pastors to conform to the political and ideological goals of national socialism. Amid the tension, a young (early thirties, yet wise-beyond-his-years) German theologian and pastor named Dietrich Bonhoeffer recognized the immense challenge that lay ahead for those who aligned with the Confessing Church movement. Because the confessing churches and their leaders sought to stay true to the Bible and church creeds, they were viewed by the Nazis as a resistance organization.[1]

Early in 1939, Bonhoeffer (who had lived, studied, and taught in America from the summer of 1930 to the summer of 1931) was forced to wrestle with a major decision. He had received a letter requiring men his age to register for military service under the leadership of the führer. Dietrich had three options: he could register, which his conscience and convictions simply would not allow him to do; he could be a conscientious objector to the National Socialist cause, which would bring major scrutiny upon the whole Confessing Church and likely conclude with him imprisoned; or he could have his call-up deferred one year and potentially return to America and work in a burgeoning ecumenical movement.

After much prayer and wise counsel from Christian leaders throughout Europe and in America, Bonhoeffer boarded the *Bremen* en route to America. Through the invitation of his former seminary professor Reinhold Niebuhr, Dietrich would teach and lecture in the United States. He would also serve to faithfully communicate the struggles of the Confessing Church movement in Germany to a broader audience.

His stay in America was brief.

Bonhoeffer wrestled with his decision to leave Germany from the moment his ship set sail for New York. And it only got worse the longer he stayed in the States. He *had* to return to Germany!

Less than one month after arriving in America, Bonhoeffer wrote to Niebuhr:

> I have come to the conclusion that I have made a mistake in coming to America. I must live through this difficult period of our national history with the Christian people of Germany. I shall have no right to participate in the reconstruction of Christian life in Germany after the war if I do not share the trials of this time with my people.[2]

In late July of 1939, Bonhoeffer returned to an unsettled, volatile, and dangerous Germany.

Dietrich didn't have to thrust himself into the heart of the political and spiritual tornado that was Nazi Germany. He chose to be there. He chose to return and fight for truth, justice, and God's church.

The ultimate cost of Bonhoeffer's sacrificial service to God's people—his life.[3]

Dietrich Bonhoeffer's sacrifice for God's people has become iconic. His bravery in the face of immense struggle and danger has made him a hero to many Christ followers worldwide. Yet it's not fair (or realistic) for us to look at Bonhoeffer's life and quietly think, "Yeah, I should be more bold and courageous like Bonhoeffer was in the face of immense trials." This is not why I'm using Bonhoeffer's sacrificial service as an illustration. Instead, I'm seeking to help God's people recognize that his decision to return to Germany to serve God's people amid great pending trials exhibited three critical things that every Christ follower must consider when serving. Bonhoeffer's service was Christ-centered, others-focused, and church-strengthening.

Service: A Response to the Servant

Service was the reason Jesus left the perfect communion he experienced with his Father and the Holy Spirit to live among his creation. Jesus entered into our world with a heart of service. He made this very clear as he spoke to his disciples: "For even the Son of Man came not to be served but to serve, and to give his life as a ransom for many" (Mark 10:45).

Spend a few moments thinking about *that*! Seriously. Consider the God of creation, the God of heaven and earth, the God of Adam and Eve, entering into our world to become a servant to those who had sinned against him. The ones that he knew would shun, beat, bruise, mock, spit upon, and ultimately crucify him. The Holy One came to sacrificially serve unholy ones like you and me. This truth alone should drop us to our knees faster than an Easton baseball bat powerfully swung at our shins. Does it? Does the truth of God coming to earth as a servant even register a blip on the radar screen of our minds? Or is it just some far-off religious idea that you heard in a Sunday school class when you were young? Some nice, feel-good church story that has no real bearing on your faith journey today?

As followers of this servant King, we should sense deeply the impact of this reality. Not simply because Jesus gave us a nice model to follow. It's much more than that. Numerous people throughout human history have given later generations nice moral examples to emulate. This is different. Much different. This is the God-man. This is Jesus. This is the Christ. His sacrificial service, both in his earthly life and in his brutal death, is the gospel!

The royal and regal King came to serve dirty and diseased peasants. This King was supremely wise, so he knew these simple, ignorant peasants would one day turn on him, shame him, and kill him. This King came to lavish love upon them and sacrificially serve them anyway. And these acts of service changed everything.

I am one of the many peasants who have been served by this King. Through his sacrificial service I am humbled. I am embarrassed. I am honored. I am dumbfounded. I am grateful. I am bewildered. I am brought to my knees in worship. I am changed!

The sacrificial service that Jesus's model established should ultimately transform the actions of all who follow him. However, acts of service for imitation's sake are not where we should begin. Christ followers must begin with a head and heart engagement with this servant King. We must recognize and seek to understand the tremendous cost that Jesus paid to serve his people. The magnitude of Jesus's sacrificial service must penetrate our mind and pierce our heart. Then, and only then, will this transformation cause our hands to become active in response to God's sacrificial service and amazing grace for us. Our hands begin to serve not to earn the favor of this royal and regal King—he's already come to serve me—but, rather, out of a deep love and gratitude for the way he has already served me.

> The magnitude of Jesus's sacrificial service must penetrate our mind and pierce our heart.

Coauthors Matt Chandler, Josh Patterson, and Eric Geiger capture the force of Christ's first serving us: "The foundation

of our service is built upon Christ's birth, life, death, and resurrection for us. It begins and ends with Jesus—*begins* there
because He is our original motivation and *ends* there because
only in Him are we empowered to serve."[4]

If Jesus came to earth simply to model a good moral life and
give us a few random acts of kindness, then the only necessary response for a believer would be done with our hands.
We would follow his example by performing sacrificial acts
of service and then be done. No further effect. There would
be nothing given away but a temporary counterfeit feeling of
goodness. But that's not all that Jesus was, nor was it all that
his sacrificial service sought to accomplish.

The apostle Paul understood this important distinction
clearly. This is why he taught the churches in Galatia to use the
freedom they had in Christ as the foundation from which they
would serve. Paul writes, "For you were called to freedom,
brothers. Only do not use your freedom as an opportunity for
the flesh, but through love serve one another" (Gal. 5:13).

Genuine head and heart knowledge of the servant King
gives freedom. Freedom to serve others with your actions. This
service is a direct response to the freedom that you have because of what Jesus did to serve you and to set you free.

"Freedom, then, sets the stage for service," writes Sittser.
"Gratitude for God's gifts will inspire us to use our gifts for
others; freedom from compulsion will make us eager to sacrifice for somebody else's sake."[5]

As you breathe in the fresh air of this freedom, you are then
free to assist others. It's similar to the directions we're given by
our flight attendants every time we board an aircraft. It goes
something like this: "In case of a loss of cabin pressure, an
oxygen mask will fall down from the overhead compartment.
Please secure your own oxygen mask first before helping others." Frankly, I've always found these directions to be a bit

selfish, almost rude. Not so. The reason we must secure our oxygen masks first is that we have just 15–20 seconds before we would experience confusion and a euphoric state, likely forgetting everything we were told earlier by our flight attendant. Within 30–40 seconds we would probably pass out.[6] So it's imperative that we secure our own oxygen before assisting others. Similarly, we Christ followers must first secure our own head and heart understanding of service before we can begin to put our hands into action assisting others.

The Freedom to Serve Sacrificially

From this position of freedom, my head and my heart are set upon God. Then my focus turns to others, and finally toward myself. Unless this three-tiered order is in place in my own head and heart, any service I give to another will be an internal struggle against my own will, my own needs, and my own desires.

Jesus understood the internal struggle that we would experience. He knew man's heart so well that he spoke directly about this issue when facing the critical questioning of the Pharisees.

> "Teacher, which is the great commandment in the Law?" And he said to him, "You shall love the Lord your God with all your heart and with all your soul and with all your mind. This is the great and first commandment. And a second is like it: You shall love your neighbor as yourself." (Matt. 22:36–39)

Clearly, Jesus desires, even commands, the heart of a believer to be submitted—first to God, then to the love of our neighbor. To see my neighbor's will, my neighbor's needs, and my neighbor's desires as I see my own. This is the heart of service, and this is incredibly difficult! Our default mode is to want the biggest, nicest, and most of everything in life. My heart wants the biggest piece of pizza at the party. My heart yearns to have the nicest house on the block. My heart longs for the most possible money in my bank account. This is why Jesus addressed this heart problem succinctly.

First-century Christians not only understood Jesus's teaching about their neighbors; they put it into practice in radically selfless ways. When one among them had a need, others would sacrifice their own personal property to take care of their brother or sister in the community (Acts 4:34–35).

Certainly, the world is a different place today. The community of Christ's followers is now scattered all over the world. Some believers have much. Other believers have tremendous needs. For those of us with much, we can learn plenty from our first-century brethren about sacrificing what we call "ours" for the greater needs of other believers.

I witnessed the importance of this type of sacrifice when I went to Haiti last summer. Our group of middle-class American believers visited the homes of two children who are sponsored by Compassion International. The entire residence for a family of eight was not much bigger than a common American living room. Yet, a monthly sponsorship provided each sponsored child with regular meals, immunizations, clothes, and consistent opportunities to hear the gospel. These are opportunities that other non-sponsored children simply do not have.

Many on our team met their sponsored child face-to-face for the first time. They witnessed and heard firsthand stories of the dramatic impact of their monthly financial sacrifice.[7] All of us who met our sponsored children actually came away wanting to do more for them. Every one of us! To sacrifice more money, to invest more time writing them letters, and to spend more time in prayer on their behalf. It was plain for us all to recognize that our small sacrifice is a huge gift to those who receive it. We have so much. So we sacrificially give to those who do not. This is the way God intended it to be among his people.

It's about the One Being Served

Service is really a simple concept; it's serving another who is in need. It's placing someone else's needs above my own. It's doing something that I may not like, enjoy, tell my friends about, or post on Facebook. Service is simply not about me, my happiness, my joy, my status, or my ability to cultivate a heartwarming story that I might one day tell others. At its core, service is about whom I am serving. Period.

The apostle Paul also addressed the importance of considering others before self when he wrote to the saints in Philippi: "Do nothing from rivalry or conceit, but in humility count others more significant than yourselves. Let each of you look not only to his own interests, but also to the interests of others" (Phil. 2:3–4).

This exhortation strikes, once again, at the head and the heart of the Christ follower. It's not simply about my hands going through the motions of some well-intended acts of generosity. It's about my head and my heart being in agreement that the needs of others are of greater concern than my own. My fellow Christ follower's pain hurts more than my pain. My fellow believers' crisis is more significant than a crisis of my own.

Again, this is not something that comes easily. It's a challenge from the apostle Paul that, if we're honest, leaves us questioning, "What about my needs? What about my concerns? What about my . . . ?"

Paul's thinking here is brilliant. He challenges an entire community of believers to consider others first. In doing so, who has the responsibility of having your best interest and well-being in mind? Everyone does.

Now, let's consider for a moment: what if Paul had challenged the entire community to be self-centered, self-serving, self-sufficient? Imagine the outcome if Paul had written, "Let each of you look only to your own interests," and then stopped. Who would have the responsibility of your best interest and well-being then? You would. You'd be on your own. The community of God's people would not be there to love you, encourage you, or serve you. There'd be no community at all!

Instead, when we follow Paul's exhortation and strive to place greater significance on others, each individual in the community benefits. Everyone has someone to serve, and everyone has someone to serve him or her. It's not just the person with the most talent or the most resources who benefits.

But striving to put others' needs before my own is hard work. Getting to this point on a head and heart level is tough enough (as we've already discussed), but then we must strive to overcome the practical, tangible, day-to-day challenges of living this out.

Two primary challenges face all of us. First, there's time. Who has enough of it? Who has any extra time that they're eagerly seeking to give away? Nobody I know. Our own pace ties our hands of service behind our back. Our own busy, crazy, hectic lifestyles are an enemy of service. Our head and our heart may lead us to the edge of service, but our busyness drives us backward. Next is our own lack of intentionality. If we are not seeking to serve, it likely won't happen. We'll *hope* to serve. We'll *wish* that we had served. We'll convince ourselves that someday we *will* serve. But service won't happen unless we pursue specific service opportunities. Sittser correctly acknowledges, "If service is not planned, it's the first thing to go when our time is pinched."[8]

> If we are not seeking to serve, it likely won't happen.

Using the Gifts That God Has Given You

So, who gets hurt the most when God's people fail to overcome self-centeredness, busyness, and/or lack of planning to serve? The church does. The church remains underserved, under-developed, and under-resourced by the gifts that God has given each Christ follower when we are not serving (1 Cor. 12:4–11; 1 Pet. 4:10). The community of God's people suffers when I am not putting into action the gift(s) that I have been given.

"Our gifts are meant to be shared in community, for they flourish in relationship to others," writes Rick McKinley. "Without relationship these gifts turn inward and move us into self-love, and we begin to worship ourselves again. Our gifts can become idols, but in the context of community our gifts are just that—gifts. They are gifts from God to us, for us to give away for others to enjoy."[9]

This raises questions we must all ask ourselves: What's my gift? How am I to be serving God by serving his people?

Is it hospitality? Are you called to offer a home-cooked meal to a family who's just lost a loved one? Or perhaps provide a warm bed and soft blanket to a fellow believer in need of a short-term place to rest?

Is it administration? Has God given you the ability to think clearly and lead the implementation of all the details necessary to organize a large event at your church? Or perhaps to offer your gift to a local school that is in dire need of structure and direction?

Is it giving? Has God blessed you with an abundance of financial resources that you're called to wisely give to support the work of a missionary couple who is taking God's truth to unreached or restricted-access areas around the world? Or perhaps assist a young person through college or seminary? Or possibly help your church build a new student center that will shape the lives of teens throughout your city?

Is it mercy? Has God given you a tender and empathetic heart toward people who are suffering so that you can comfort them in the midst of their pain? Or perhaps serve a lonely person in your neighborhood who battles mental illness?

These quick examples are just a small sample of the gifts that God has given his people to bring himself glory (1 Pet. 4:11).[10] The question all Christ followers must engage with is how intentional are we about putting our gifts into action? How many of our gifts are being shelved because we're too absorbed in our own day-to-day struggles? How many of our gifts are going unused because our busy twenty-first-century lifestyle requires more of us than we can handle? How many of our gifts are getting rusty because we are not intentional about seeking people whom we can serve?

I know; that's a lot of questions. Probably too many questions for most of us to casually consider without having to make dramatic changes in our lives. But in order for the unfinished church to be the finished church that God intends for us to become, dramatic change serving others might be exactly what God is asking of us.

STRENGTHENING GOD'S CHURCH

Each spring and fall, many of the small groups at our church voluntarily choose to serve the elderly and widowed members of our congregation who have asked for assistance in getting their homes ready for the upcoming summer and winter weather. Weeds are pulled, yards are raked, flower beds are prepared, windows are washed, and garages get organized. This has proved to be a great marriage between the person who needs the assistance and a group of eight to fourteen adults (and sometimes their children) willing to sacrifice their time to give the assistance.

Many churches, large and small, challenge the members

of their congregation to this type of service, because it helps create a culture of awareness. It helps shine a spotlight on the basic needs in any community. And it plants the seed of expectation to those within a congregation.

This is what nonbelievers expect to see from God's people. Love lived out through serving one another. Lives characterized by service of each other. If we don't care, comfort, support, and serve our own people, how much has the radical nature of a holy King coming to earth to serve these people really changed you and me? What difference does the gospel really make if my life is not marked by service for the King who came to serve his people?

But don't be too quick to confine serving one another to inside the typical local church bubble. Serving God by serving others takes on many forms—both within the church and outside the walls of your building. It's done each Sunday when the body of Christ gathers to celebrate in community with choirs and worship teams, with greeters and ushers, with communion preparers and prayer teams. It's done in the civic setting when Christ followers serve soup at the homeless shelter, read books with children at the local elementary school's reading program, and handle all of the administration for the community 5K road race.

While some may not see this wide array of mundane tasks as God-honoring, church-building service, I love what David Augsburger suggests: "Every act of caring, support, confrontation, and healing truth-telling is a form of service and therefore an act of worship. It is done to and for the neighbor as a recognition that we stand before and in the presence of God."[11]

Service is a mom sitting beside the bed of her child who can't sleep. It's a dad taking an overtime shift to earn a few extra dollars so his kids can go on the school field trip. It's a grandmother writing letters and sending an occasional care package to her grandson at college. It's a youth pastor showing up to watch one of his students play a JV baseball game. It's a teacher who stays after school to work with the student who's struggling and doesn't have academic support at home. All are forms of service that, when done because the servant King first served you, will bring honor to God and ultimately help to build and strengthen his church.

At the end of his book *The Living Church*, longtime pastor and prominent theologian John Stott casts a beautiful vision for what the church can be if we serve God, one another, and our community well.

> I have a dream of a church which is *a serving church*—
> which has seen Christ as the Servant
> and has heard his call to be a servant too,
> which is delivered from self-interest,
> turned inside out,
> and giving itself selflessly to the service of others,
> whose members obey Christ's commands
> to live in the world,
> to permeate secular society,
> to be the salt of the earth and the light of the world . . . .
> I have a dream of a serving church.[12]

Stott's dream is an attainable reality. Certainly if we are Christ followers, we can humble ourselves before God, and before our brothers and sisters in faith, to serve each other. Certainly we can begin to see the basic needs of others as more important than our own nonessential "needs." Certainly we can find the deep needs within our local community, roll up our sleeves in service, and make a difference. I believe that it's possible, but only if we engage the servant King with our head and with our heart. Then, by doing so, we can offer up our hands of service to God, submitting ourselves to whatever service he has given us to do.

This is a serving church—a church that brings God glory.

Church History

The truths discussed in this chapter have deep roots in the history of God's church. Consider the following example as you engage with these truths.

THE WESTMINSTER CONFESSION OF FAITH

Chapter XXVI. Of the Communion of the Saints

2. Saints by profession are bound to maintain an holy fellowship and communion in the worship of God, and in performing such other spiritual services as tend to their mutual edification; as also in relieving each other in outward things according to their several abilities and necessities. Which communion, as God offereth opportunity, is to be extended unto all those who, in every place, call upon the name of the Lord Jesus.[13]

Music

The themes discussed in this chapter have been expressed in both traditional and contemporary music. Below are a few titles to encourage you as you reflect on these themes.

"The Servant King," by Graham Kendrick
"Humble King," by Brenton Brown
"Hearts of Servants" (Shane and Shane), by Shane Barnard
"My Own Little World," by Matthew West

Questions for Discussion

These questions have been developed for you to consider personally, answer honestly, and discuss openly—engaging your head and your heart—as you process the truths of this chapter together in community.

1. Read Mark 10:42–45. Meditate on it. Describe your thoughts and your emotions about Jesus coming not to be served but to serve.

2. How does the freedom you have in Christ affect the way you view service? And as you engage with this truth, how might it change how you serve in the days ahead? Explain with a tangible example.

3. Engaging with the servant King on a head and heart level before putting your hands into action was a major theme of this chapter. Discuss why this is so important.

4. In Philippians 2:3–4, Paul exhorts the people of God to look at the interests of others instead of simply looking at their own. Consider for a moment if Paul had instead written, "Let each of you look only to your own interests." Would your life look any different? Describe any potential differences.

5. Two primary obstacles to serving were discussed in this chapter: time and intentionality. Which of these is the bigger obstacle to your service? Is there another obstacle that you struggle with? Discuss.

6. Do you know your spiritual gifts? How are you currently using them in serving others? Explain with examples.

7

Dwell in Unity

Jesus Loves His Church, So You Should Too

Behold, how good and pleasant it is when brothers dwell in unity.

> Psalm 133:1

There are Christians who say, "I love God but I hate the church." But they are members all the same, whether they like it or not, whether they acknowledge it or not.

> Eugene Peterson, *A Long Obedience in the Same Direction*

And what makes us think that after nearly two thousand years of institutional church, Christians are suddenly free to jettison the church and try things on their own?

> Kevin DeYoung, *Why We Love the Church*

It was a typical church library. Lots of bookshelves. Plenty of old titles. A few relic teaching series on VHS tape. A rarely used commentary set. A smattering of round tables. And some marginal coffee.

This was the backdrop for one of the most troubling and telling discussions I've been a part of in recent years. A collection of roughly twenty-five Christ followers from all walks

126

of life, from all parts of our city, from all different churches and denominations, brought together by a mutual friend of everyone in the room. His goal was to dialogue about God's church—the good, the not-so-good, and the potential for partnership in serving the community in the days ahead.

Also joining the discussion was an "outsider." Not because of his personal faith—he's a believer—but because he wasn't from our city. Dan Merchant, an independent filmmaker from the Pacific Northwest who came to town to discuss his most successful film project, *Lord, Save Us from Your Followers*,[1] at the local community college, entered into the lively discussion.

What happened in the church library next caught me more than a bit off guard. As we went around the room introducing ourselves, a handful of people spoke up about their deep angst toward the church. I'm not referring to a slightly underhanded comment or an under-the-breath bash. I'm talking vitriol. Pain. Anger. The comments were direct. They were communicated with passion, a touch of mockery, and a large dose of sarcasm. Their statements lacked even a hint of grace or compassion toward the church.[2] These people either had been or were currently being deeply wounded by God's church.

Since I'm a pastor and someone who loves the church, the dialogue stirred plenty of raw emotions of my own. I found myself emotionally grieved, intellectually curious, and doctrinally frustrated. Why the angst? Who in the church wounded this man so deeply that it's become easy for him to cast aside the entire thing? What is there in this woman's past that could ignite a spark of frustration toward the church that burns so hot? I was so taken aback by the intensity of the church loathing that I confess to being rendered almost speechless.

My experience is not abnormal. If we are listening to the sidewalk conversations or paying attention to the research,[3] these antichurch discussions are taking place across the country—frequently. It's happening in the heartland and in big cities. It's young men and middle-aged women. It's burned-out church leaders and people who haven't set foot inside a local congregation in a decade.

What all the polls are showing is that Jesus is popular. People like him. He's cool. His church? Well, that's another story.

A Troubling Narrative

The "I love Jesus, but I hate the church" narrative has become commonplace within the Christian culture today. Library shelves of books[4] and articles[5] have been written about the issue. Facebook posts and tweets touting this antichurch brand of Christianity are rampant. And for the most part, it has become increasingly accepted as a viable option on the smorgasbord of living out your Christian faith. "As long as you love Jesus," many in our culture say, "you're good!"

Really? This is biblical faith? This is a faith lived out according to the Scriptures?

Many Christ followers have painful, embarrassing, confusing, weird, and downright dreadful stories of their personal experience with the church. Some have been wounded by the organization that is the church, and others have been hurt and cast aside by the people who make up the local congregation. Both can be ugly. Both can create wounds and scars. But the decision to cast the church aside as if it is some ancillary product of Christianity is simply not a biblical option. In practice, you cannot simply create an equation of I + Jesus = Authentic Christian Life, and say that you're living out biblical Christianity.

The decision to cast the church aside as if it is some ancillary product of Christianity is simply not a biblical option.

The apostle Paul explained the heart of unity among believers when he wrote to the saints in Ephesus, "There is one body and one Spirit . . . one Lord, one faith, one baptism, one God and Father of all, who is over all and through all and in all" (Eph. 4:4–6). The very foundation of the church is built upon the Trinitarian God we worship and serve. There is one Spirit. There is one Lord. There is one God and Father. And through faith in this Trinity—we are one. We are one body. We experience one baptism. And this Trinity is over all, through all, and in all. The Trinity cannot be separated. "The underlying and all-encompassing oneness that is church flows from the underlying and all-encompassing oneness that is God," writes Eugene Peterson.[6]

Because of the oneness of God, and our being welcomed into communion with this Trinity, we enter into relationships with other members of this body covered in the grace of God. As we are in relationship with the Trinity—we are one. Period. How is it then that those of us who have faith and are welcomed into this body think that we can remove ourselves? How can a God-fearing, Bible-believing, Jesus-T-shirt-wearing, *ichthus*-symbol-bearing Christ follower just take his Bible and go home? Good question, without a solid answer. It's not right thinking; rather it's wrong believing.

PROBLEMS, PROBLEMS, PROBLEMS

Certainly there are many obvious challenges facing the church today: the gospel of prosperity, which suggests that if I follow Jesus faithfully, he'll bless me financially; liberal theology, which has taken hold of some entire denominations, moving them away from the centrality of the gospel and God's inspired Word; the politicizing of American Christianity, which has brought our ancient faith into contemporary political issues as a weapon instead of a tool for good; and the social-justice gospel, which has taken Christ's actions as a model to serve without marrying word and deed ministry like the Savior did—just to name a few. These are all big-picture challenges rooted in doctrinal error or manipulation of the Scriptures to fit a certain ideology.

I don't care for these aspects of the contemporary church today either. In fact, I don't like them at all! But to make the church the fall guy for the faulty, misguided beliefs or perspectives of a select few who claim the name of Christ is like selling your car because the radio doesn't work. It's a hasty, shortsighted, knee-jerk reaction. And one more thing; it's not biblical!

Problems will arise within our body, within our oneness. Problems caused by us, and problems caused by others. Problems that are avoidable, and problems that are unavoidable. Problems due to the sin of commission, and problems due to the sin of omission. Problems. Issues. Situations. Struggles. They arise among God's people. Christ followers are not, nor have we ever been, exempt from intense challenges.

One chapter from the Psalms, specifically from a group of psalms known as the Songs of Ascents (Psalms 120–34), helps us find a measure of normalcy amid the problems and issues we face inside our community of oneness. Here's the setting behind the words of David. The people of God are making their annual pilgrimage to Jerusalem for festival worship. As they journey together, they sing these words joyously:

> Behold, how good and pleasant it is
>   when brothers dwell in unity!
> It is like the precious oil on the head,
>   running down on the beard,
> on the beard of Aaron,
>   running down on the collar of his robes! . . .
> For there the Lord has commanded the blessing,
>   life evermore. (Psalm 133)

In this rich chapter of Scripture, a couple things are either so obvious or loaded with so much imagery that we have to give them special attention or we'll miss their significance.

First is the subtle acknowledgment that brothers (and sisters) sometimes do not get along. That's why David makes a point to communicate the goodness and peace, "Behold, how good and pleasant it is," that is experienced when brothers (and sisters) actually do get along. It doesn't happen often,[7] so when it does it's a powerful thing!

Second, is the rich imagery that oozes from the word picture that David gives us of oil running through Aaron's long beard. Throughout Scripture oil is used as a symbol of God's presence and favor. Oil shines. It softens. It carries a pleasant aroma as it is often mixed with many fragrant spices. It has a richness that is conveyed to the senses of both touch and smell. Also important is the reality that oil was also used to set apart a priest as anointed (Lev. 8:30). The imagery in Psalm 133 gives this marking to the brothers (and sisters) as fellow priests to one another. We see this spelled out more clearly in the New Testament when Peter addresses all Christ followers as priests (1 Pet. 2:9).

Peterson understands well the significance of David's use of imagery in this Song of Ascents: "Living together means seeing the oil flow over the head, down the face, through the beard, onto the shoulders of the other—and when I see that I know that my brother, my sister, is my priest. When we see the other as God's anointed, our relationships are profoundly affected."[8]

Do you see your brother (or sister) in faith this way? Do you see the person you sit beside each week in your small group this way? How about your children's Sunday school teacher? How about your next-door neighbor who loves Jesus but happens to worship at a different church?

The Construction

Is Your Theology Your Prison?

Let's be brutally honest; it takes some intentional effort to get to the place where you are truly able to see those who attend different churches, read different authors, and listen to different preachers than you do as your priests.

Denominations are an easy excuse for the separation that exists. But other, less formal divisions also keep us from experiencing much unity:

- Worship style: contemporary worship, traditional hymns, or a blended service
- Preaching methodology: expository teaching or topical sermons
- Outreach ideology: word evangelism, deed-based mercy ministry, or some combination of both

These items are nonessential, peripheral, preference issues. What do I prefer? What is the best approach? What meets my needs? Truth is, these are not issues that should separate one Christ follower from another. They may stir some intriguing dialogue—and if you're really passionate about a particular hot-button issue, things could even escalate into a friendly debate. But these are not the essential issues that should cause us to draw an imaginary line in the sand.

There is a phrase from church history that has served believers well throughout many different shifts in the theological landscape. It has proved to be a timeless and clear call for unity among Christ followers. The phrase reads, "In essentials unity, in non-essentials liberty, in all things charity." Although typically attributed to Saint Augustine, scholar and professor Mark Ross suggests it was delivered by someone less well known.

It comes from an otherwise undistinguished German Lutheran theologian of the early seventeenth century,

Rupertus Meldenius. The phrase occurs in a tract on Christian unity written (c. 1627) during the Thirty Years War (1618–1648), a bloody time in European history in which religious tensions played a significant role.[9]

Referred to as "the watchword of Christian peacemakers" by nineteenth-century church historian Philip Schaff,[10] the phrase is still being used by denominations and churches today as their official motto. It offers a clear framework in which God's people can process their beliefs and practices. It lifts the core doctrines (virgin birth, sacrificial death, bodily resurrection, etc.) of the historic Christian faith higher than issues that are not gospel-centric (age of the earth, view of end times, etc.), and it reminds us to be gracious and love well regardless of the issue.

As a Christ follower, I have many personal convictions about biblical truth, theology, and the way in which I practice my faith. So do you. So does everyone else. Some of my beliefs are better thought out than others. Some of my convictions are strong on certain issues, while I may be a bit less strident on some others. This is where I must personally engage with Meldenius's challenge. My biblical and theological understanding serves as my foundation. From this base, my foundational understanding, I build and develop all that I teach and practice in real life. My foundation, however, is not a cold, barren, barred prison cell. It does not lock me in and block my vision of others. My biblical and theological base does not, and should not, prohibit me from listening to, loving, encouraging, or serving those whose foundation is different from my own.

Mark Buchanan describes the value in cutting across such barriers.

> On many matters, we have not equality, or want it, or seek it. But on deep matters, we have oneness. Differences of

opinion serve only to enliven rather than undermine our friendship. They make for fun banter. They spice and vary our conversations, keeping our relationship from staleness and blandness. We need only to agree with one another in the Lord.[11]

Regularly Worshipping at the Church of the Mirror

Achieving this sort of Christ-centered, essential-seeking unity just might be the biggest challenge facing the church today. Denominational, theological, and practical differences separate believers every day in unimaginable ways. Episcopalian and Pentecostal worship styles couldn't be more different. The Armenians and the Calvinists just can't seem to agree on much when it comes to doctrinal issues. And all the Christians who vote Republican because of the pro-life issue just can't see eye to eye on the social-justice position of those believers who vote for the Democratic ticket.

Unfortunately, these major-category differences drive us to opposite corners of an imaginary sparring ring. We squeeze on our denominational gloves, throw on our theological headgear, lace up our practical shoes, and start sparring with each other. Think about it for a minute: when was the last time you saw an Episcopalian church and a Pentecostal church partner together on any significant ministry in your city? When was the last time Arminians and Calvinists came together to celebrate the doctrinal beliefs that they *do* hold in common? And when was the last time the conservative Christian group and the more liberal leaning Christians got together to put the love of Jesus into action serving side by side?

These sorts of things don't typically happen because they don't *need* to happen. Almost any Christian group (fill in the name of your denomination, theological camp, or favorite parachurch organization) is so well resourced—with funds and/or people—that it has little need for groups who view things differently.

Individual Christ followers like you and me are really no different. There just isn't any real need to try very hard for unity. We have more spiritual-growth options at our disposal than one of those new mix-everything Coke machines offers in soda selections. "You want Raspberry Coke? You've got it! Or was it Cherry Vanilla Coke? Yeah, that's it." Technology has afforded us more choices than we could ever possibly have time for, and the most intriguing thing is that the choices cost the individual Christ follower nothing more than a little bit of time, a laptop or tablet, and a high-speed Internet connection.

> Who needs the local church when I can have my sermons, my music, and my community the way I want them?

Consider the options:

- Don't like the messages that your pastor delivers? Simply download the latest sermon from your favorite "famous" pastor, courtesy of his church's website. Drink from the well of the gifted!
- Don't care for the worship style of your local congregation? No problem, just grab the latest songs from your favorite worship artist (or band) off iTunes, and create your own playlist for Jesus. Crank up *your* Jesus tunes and truly enter into worship!
- Don't like the people sitting next to you at church? Can't seem to connect? Just jump online and connect with your Facebook "friends" for some spiritually stimulating dialogue. Instant community without all the messiness!

Who needs the local church when I can have my sermons, my music, and my community the way I want them? At the

Church of the Mirror there is no conflict. No struggle. No disagreement. And no real need for unity. Why bother? I can have it all!

Jessie Rice captures the problem at the center of this thinking.

> We'd rather be consumers of relationships—taking the parts we want and leaving out the parts we don't—than face dealing with all of home's demands (and benefits). And so, unfortunately, we scratch our heads and wonder why we can't seem to find the kind of community experience we're looking for, all the while remaining willfully adolescent in our relational habits.[12]

There is precious little humility in the Church of the Mirror. There is very little asking. Little listening. Little understanding. And even less forgiveness. When the church spins on the axis of me—my needs, wants, preferences, and all-important opinions—there is little room for anyone else. Especially someone who doesn't agree with the views represented in my mirror—because those views are deeper than they appear.

Don't Talk about My Bride That Way!

One of my mentors is professor, author, and radio Bible teacher Steve Brown. While I was in seminary, Steve taught me much about the church. He shared stories about the church that would take your breath away, stories that would bring you to your knees in repentance, and stories that would bring tears of shame and disgust to your eyes. As a pastor for more than twenty years, Steve has seen and experienced the entire spectrum of life in the church.

Yet, Steve loves the church! He often jokes with his seminary students that he doesn't always *like* the church, but he does *love* God's church deeply.[13] That's why I appreciate the honest words Steve shared on one of his radio broadcasts: "Every time I go to God [in prayer] and complain about the church, and I do it often, and I tell him about the bad stuff, he says, 'I know. But you be careful, because that's my wife.'"[14]

The biblical truth that Steve wryly mentions is the primary reason that angst-filled comments about the church are so troubling. According to Scripture, the church is the bride of Christ (Eph. 5:25–27; Rev. 19:7–9). When we speak poorly of the church, we're speaking of Jesus's bride. Think about that for a moment. Our condemning and hurtful comments directed at the church are addressed to the bride of our Savior. Do you suppose that Jesus is just fine with our angst? Do you believe he's happy about the insults we so casually hurl at his bride? Do you think he says: "Go ahead, fire away! Whatever you say is probably true. She's a loser. I never really loved her all that much anyway?" Any man that I know who has even a small amount of love, respect, care, or concern for his wife would be appalled!

The hypocrisy and judgment the church has shown to many people certainly are not very becoming of a bride. Nor are the lack of grace for her own people and the insistence on always being right very attractive. She may be the bride of Jesus, but everyone can agree that she's certainly not very pleasant at times.

Kevin DeYoung acknowledges the truth of the bride's flaws. But he also recognizes a great deal of irony in the actions of her accusers.

> The church will be full of sin so long as she is full of sinners—which is kind of the point I thought. It's more than a little ironic that the same folks who want the church to ditch the phony, plastic persona and become a haven for broken, imperfect sinners are ready to leave the church when she is broken, imperfect, and sinful.[15]

The intriguing twist that I see in the "I love Jesus, but I hate the church" narrative is the two primary charges thrown at the bride of Christ—a judgmental spirit and a lack of forgiveness—are the very issues that lie at the heart of the angst people have with the church. First, a spirit of judgment toward what the church hasn't been, hasn't done, and ought to be doing. Next, a spirit that lacks forgiveness for the grievances the church has intentionally and unintentionally done to its people.

The pent-up anger and frustration directed at the church often begins with one big offense or a series of smaller offenses, wounds, or attacks that go undisclosed and/or unforgiven. Over time, these offenses develop deep, twisted, tangled roots in the hearts and minds of the wounded. Bitterness has found a home. And it won't easily go away.

But there is a solution—forgiveness.

Forgiveness is that thing that you and I received through Jesus's sacrificial death on the cross. It's that thing that once set us free from the penalty of our own sin. Now, it is the only thing that can set us free from the tangled roots of bitterness, resentment, frustration, and anger toward Christ's bride. We are called to offer it to others. "As the Lord has forgiven you, so you also must forgive" (Col. 3:13).

> Forgiveness is exactly what is required of us if unity is to be experienced in the church.

Actually, Jesus does more than call us to offer forgiveness to others. He requires it of his followers. "For if you forgive others their trespasses, your heavenly Father will also forgive you, but if you do not forgive others their trespasses, neither will your Father forgive your trespasses" (Matt. 6:14–16).

Why the requirement? Why must we do this hard thing? Why does God ask the heart-wrenching task of forgiving someone who has harmed us? Honest questions for a hard truth. If we cannot forgive the sins of those who have wronged or wounded us, we clearly have not understood the significance of our own transgressions against God. The grace and mercy of God is lost on us.

Perhaps this forgiveness stuff seems like a nice, trite, religious solution. Or perhaps it's the opposite—it just seems far too difficult. Perhaps what Jesus teaches us in the gospel is just too hard to live out. Your pain is just too intense. Your wound is just too deep. These are honest and very real emotions. Yet, forgiveness is exactly what is required of us if unity is to be experienced in the church.

Marva Dawn details the effort that's required.

> The unity of the community of faith requires practice.
>
> That practice might involve some confrontation, but that, too, is an important lesson about the unity of the Church that we must learn. . . .
>
> . . . God's Spirit is at work in us to make us into the community of Christ, but the sandpaper of our relationships grinds down the rough spots.[16]

Former political lightning rod turned Christ follower Chuck Colson adds a level of time and intensity to Dawn's requirement. Colson writes, "It takes time to develop unity with others at any depth, and this never takes place, ever—not at any time or anywhere—without conflict."[17]

Forgiveness, confrontation, time, and conflict—together they make a daunting list of why unity is so difficult to find among God's people today. It requires hard heart-work and plenty of humility to make it happen. And when you finally get there, you're only half of the equation. The other members of God's church need to have done the same hard heart-work that you've done to receive and forgive you.

The faithfulness to Jesus and his Word, the selfless intro-spection and humility, and the intentionality toward another brother or sister that unity requires are among the most dif-ficult expressions of the Christian faith. Unity is very difficult! Jesus knew this would be our experience. This is precisely why our Savior made it an emphasis of his prayer to the Father in his final hours on earth.

> I am praying not only for these disciples but also for all who will ever believe in me through their message. I pray that they will be one, just as you and I are one—as you are in me, Father, and I am in you. And may they be in us so that the world will believe you sent me. I have given them the glory you gave me, so they may be one as we are one. I am in them and you are in me. May they experience such perfect unity that the world will know that you sent me and that you love them as much as you love me. (John 17:20–23, NLT)

Unity is the result of a great deal of heart-wrenching, God-seeking, others-forgiving effort. Jesus calls us to this immense personal and corporate challenge. Are you up for it? Will you see your brothers and sisters in faith as your priests? Will you do the hard heart-work? Will you practice forgiveness? The church needs you. And so does the watching world.

Church History

The truths discussed in this chapter have deep roots in the history of God's church. Consider the following example as you engage with these truths.

THE NICENE CREED

Issued in AD 325 by the First Council of Nicea, the Nicene Creed is one of the most widely accepted and broadly used creeds of the Christian faith. It was originally formulated to confront a few heresies—specifically the heresy of Gnosticism.

One line of the creed, "We believe in one holy catholic and apostolic church," is often misunderstood and seen as controversial. It need not be. The term "catholic" refers to the universality of the church. It affirms the historical, universal, body of Christ. Remember, it predates the Reformation, so it is not claiming a direct link with the Roman Catholic Church of today.

Music

The themes discussed in this chapter have been expressed in both traditional and contemporary music. Below are a couple of titles to encourage you as you reflect on these themes.

"With One Voice," by Matt Redman and Steven Curtis Chapman
"Forgiveness," by Matthew West

Questions for Discussion

These questions have been developed for you to consider personally, answer honestly, and discuss openly—engaging your head and your heart—as you process the truths of this chapter together in community.

1. Have you heard of or participated in an "I love Jesus, but I hate the church" discussion? Does it resonate with your personal experience with God's people? Or is your experience with the church something different? Explain.

2. Read Psalm 133. Discuss the power of the imagery of the oil anointing my brothers and sisters as priests. How does this heighten your view of your brothers' and sisters' importance in your life? Discuss.

3. Consider the quote "In essentials unity, in non-essentials liberty, in all things charity." How might this serve to develop greater unity with other Christ followers in your life? Explain.

4. Have you ever considered that your critical words directed at the church are being directed at Jesus's bride? How might that influence your thoughts, comments, and actions about the church?

5. For unity to become commonplace in the church, Jesus calls his followers to practice forgiveness. Discuss your level of comfort or discomfort with what Jesus asks of us.

PART 3

THE COMPLETION

8

Jesus Finishes His Building Project

As Christ loved the church and gave himself up for her, that he might sanctify her, having cleansed her by the washing of water with the word, so that he might present the church to himself in splendor.

Ephesians 5:25–26

I will build my church, and the gates of hell shall not prevail against it.

Matthew 16:18

The eternal community is the complete fulfillment of the promise running throughout the Bible, namely, that God will be present among his people.

Stanley Grenz, *Created for Community*

When I was a young boy, my parents and I would occasionally visit my aunt and uncle's home a few hours from where we lived in Michigan. My dad and his brother would spend what seemed like hours talking in my uncle's old garage. But this wasn't just any garage. My uncle's garage also served as a body shop and a paint booth. It was a place of restoration. It was the location of transportation transformation!

Whenever we would visit, my uncle would roll back the heavy wooden garage door to unveil an automotive surprise. We never knew what awaited us. Often what appeared was an eyesore to the unappreciative eye. The car would be missing familiar parts like a hood or a door, bumpers would be removed and lying off to the side of the garage, and the vehicle would be in different stages of the sanding, patching, priming, or painting process. Frankly, to a pair of school-aged eyes, the classic car undergoing restoration was just not very attractive. What I saw was a multicolored, sanded-down, dusty, unattractive piece of machinery. The body was rough. Nothing shined. It was a swirly, frosted, mess of muted colors.

Even as a boy, I knew that I was supposed to be impressed with the vintage ride that sat before my eyes. But in the car's current state, I wasn't. Structurally, the car was solid. But it wasn't right. It just wasn't how it was supposed to be, look, or perform. I couldn't see the work that had already taken place, the work that was currently being done, or the work that was still to come. I hadn't seen the damaged body or the cracked finish. I hadn't seen how my uncle had acquired the right parts and assembled key pieces to get the car to this stage of the time-consuming restoration process. I couldn't see the necessary steps that still lay ahead. The car was under construction. And I didn't have a vision for its completion.

> Sanctification is a gritty, dusty, dirty, mess of an experience.

But one day—after my uncle had purchased, pieced, patched, sanded, primed, painted, and buffed one of his many classic Corvette Stingrays—it would become a radiant, glisten-

ing, shimmering work of automotive art. It would be a thing
of beauty!

The current state of God's church is a whole lot like one
of my uncle's classic Corvettes parked behind that heavy
wooden garage door. It's a damaged body. It's cracked and
chipped. Key pieces need to be assembled. The rough spots
need to be patched and repaired. The entire body needs to
be sanded down and smoothed out. This is the process of
completion. It's a process that you and I find ourselves painfully involved in as members of God's community called the
church. And it's the process of God finishing his unfinished
church.

This process, the completion of individual Christ followers,
has a theological term; it's called sanctification. And sanctification is a gritty, dusty, dirty, mess of an experience. It's a
process that every Christ follower is going through and will
continue experiencing until God finishes the building project
of his church—every one of us. While most believers are familiar with the term *sanctification*, it is perhaps the most commonly misunderstood aspect of the faith journey.

This is tragic!

It's tragic because many of the issues we've examined in
previous chapters are rooted in our own struggle to submit to
the process of sanctification. Here's what I mean:

- Christ followers push against diversity in the body of
  Christ because we are at war in our own hearts over those
  different from us. That's a struggle to submit to the process
  of sanctification.
- We regularly fail to freely offer love to each other, because
  our own desire to be loved is so intense. That's a struggle
  to submit to the process of sanctification.
- We say that we desire unity with other Christ followers,
  yet we often avoid opportunities to develop this unity

within God's church. That's a struggle to submit to the process of sanctification.

So what is sanctification? How does it affect my personal faith journey? How do I become sanctified? There are many biblical texts that offer us details,[1] but none provides more clarity than when the apostle Paul wrote about his own faith journey to the saints in Philippi: "Not that I have already obtained this or am already perfect, but I press on to make it my own, because Christ Jesus has made me his own" (Phil. 3:12).

The power of this text is in the honest and direct way that it communicates one significant reality of sanctification. That sanctification is not justification! Justification is what Jesus has done for you on the cross, claiming you as his own. Jesus gives you his grace, his forgiveness, and his righteousness in exchange for your sin, your guilt, and your shame—once for all time. That's the meaning of the theological term *justification*—and that's very different from sanctification.

In his letter to the saints in Philippi, Paul establishes this foundational theological truth. In the heart of his letter, Paul details his own sanctification process (Phil. 3:7–16). At the end of verse 12, he explains why this whole process is even possible. It is, he says, "because Christ Jesus has made me his own." Essentially Paul is saying, "Anything I can do to become like Jesus originates from one simple truth—Jesus has made me his own!" This is the foundation of Paul's faith—and the foundation for every believer. The faith of an individual is established through the transaction of justification (Gal. 2:16). Only *after* this once-for-all exchange has taken place—Jesus's best for your worst—can the process of sanctification begin.

Unless you are first justified by Christ's sacrificial work on the cross, all of your good work, your generosity, your Bible knowledge, your correct theological viewpoints, and your trying really, really hard to be holy is done in vain. Because it's not

God-empowered, not Christ-centered, not Spirit-led—it's all worthless. No justification? No sanctification! This distinction could not be more important for the Christ follower to grasp.

Sanctification builds upon the foundation of justification. The process of sanctification is my submitting everything to Jesus. It's my bowing down at the base of Christ's cross. It's a head and heart and hands posture of total submission of everything I am and everything I want to be—to God. It's a complete surrender of my personal struggle to love well, to encourage my brothers and sisters, and to serve others. It is a total relinquishing of my will to the restorative actions of God's grace in my life.

I love the way one writer captures the process: "Sanctification is no meek and mild affair, no mere rearranging of spiritual furniture. It is an electric process, an exhilarating experience of the power of God within us. . . . As we daily believe the gospel and apply it to our lives, we taste the essence of biblical sanctification."[2]

Sanctification Matters

All this stuff about sanctification probably has you asking: Why is he writing so much about the process of sanctification in the life of a believer here in the final chapter of a book on the church? Why now? Because it is absolutely imperative that we get it, comprehend it, submit to it, believe it, receive it, and live it!

Personal sanctification may not seem all that important when you're considering it in the context of all of God's people. It may seem a bit too self-centered and not focused enough on others. It may seem far more theological than practical. Not true, on both accounts.

While most twenty-first-century Christ followers may simply be trying to live out their faith in some small way each day in a world where this is becoming increasingly difficult, passivity toward our personal sanctification is not an option. We cannot become so bored by the mundane day-to-day stuff of life that we ignore our role in God's bigger story. We must recognize that we are part of something much bigger than ourselves, bigger than our immediate family, bigger than our local congregation, and bigger than our denomination.

We are part of a movement of God that spans thousands of years and links Abraham with Augustine, doubting Thomas with Thomas Aquinas, John the Baptist with John Calvin, and Barnabas with Bonhoeffer. The body of Christ is immense in size and scope. You and I are part of a much bigger movement of God than we can see, read about, or even comprehend. Yet every believer has a significant role to play in God's grand plan for the world. This is why your personal sanctification—your personal growth into Christlikeness—is so critically important. The cumulative effect of God at work in the personal sanctification of individual Christ followers cannot be underestimated. Sanctification matters!

- It matters to the person who has been wounded by believers who were supposed to give love unconditionally, but offered judgment instead.
- It matters to the one who is in desperate need of a word of encouragement, yet never hears anything positive about his or her faith journey. Nobody seems to notice.
- It matters to the one who has needs that could be served by members of the body of Christ, but are not.
- It matters to the irritated, disgruntled, frustrated Christ follower who has almost given up on having anything to do with God's people.
- It matters to Jesus, because he desires that his followers live lives marked by love, encouragement, and service. He desires that his people live together in unity.

- It matters because Jesus's bride is bruised, beaten, battered, and bound when we passively ignore or willfully bypass opportunities for God to work in our lives.
- It matters because it requires a posture of humility before a sovereign, gracious, holy God.
- It matters because it is a tenderhearted willingness to submit to the work of the Spirit's refining work in our lives.
- It matters because it is Christ's followers being made more and more and more like the One we are following.

Sanctification matters because it is nothing less than gospel thinking, gospel believing, gospel speaking, gospel being, and gospel living!

Sanctification is the process of the Holy Spirit at work in us, changing us, sanding off the rough spots, making our lives more faithfully reflect the image of Jesus. It's the process of holy living because you're genuinely living through the power of the Holy One. J. I. Packer explains the process with great clarity: "God's method of sanctification is neither activism (self-reliant activity) nor apathy (God-reliant passivity), but God-dependent effort."[3]

This is the sort of Christ following that I want to do. I want to be submitted to God and led by the Spirit, so my brothers and sisters in faith can see God at work in me and through me—rather than watching me play some self-serving, me-honoring, religious role.

This is the Christ following that I long for my son and daughter to experience via the head, heart, and hands of their parents at home, and other Christ followers they witness while growing up.

This is the Christ following that I long to see lived out in the lives of people in my congregation, visible on the streets of my city, and spreading wildly across the globe.

This is the Christ following that I hope you have read

about, discussed with other believers in community, and been encouraged to experience from the pages of this book.

Yet, if I'm honest with myself, my desire to follow Jesus with integrity and authenticity is a very different reality from what I often live out with my actions. I may *want* others to view my comments and actions positively, but I cannot casually overlook my own missteps, failures, and moments of hypocrisy. Nor can my strongest desire to overcome the misdeeds of other Christians, other small communities of believers, local congregations, or even the large institutional church actually wipe clean the stain they have left behind. God's church has many shortcomings. (That's why much of this book offers encouragement on how to more faithfully live out the call of God on our lives.) Even a few brief moments of honest self-evaluation will help each of us see that we are in desperate need of God's sanctifying work in our own lives. And, when brought together in community, we can see with great clarity that God's people—the church—are a work-in-progress.

This truth is at the heart of DeYoung's assessment of the church.

> If we truly love the church, we will bear with her in her failings, endure her struggles, believe her to be the beloved bride of Christ, and hope for her final glorification. The church is the hope of the world—not because she gets it all right, but because she is a body with Christ for her Head.[4]

Following in Peter's Footsteps

As with the rough, rowdy, ragtag bunch of disciples that Jesus called to himself in the first century, our Lord is still using the same strategy to build his church today—bringing together humble, broken, unfinished people who are willing to follow him. This is how Jesus has been building his church from generation to generation to generation. And make no mistake—it is Jesus doing the building, and the building process is nothing short of miraculous!

About a year ago, following a Sunday morning worship service a friend introduced me to a young man named Adam. He was serving as the head of the Atheists Club at the local community college. We made friendly, casual, respectful small talk for about ten minutes. Then Adam wanted to ask me, a pastor, a few honest questions about my faith. For the next two hours, Adam and I talked with each other—in a tennis-match sort of way—about anything you could possibly imagine dealing with the Bible, theology, science, and our own personal journeys of faith. (My journey lead me to Jesus; his moved him away from God.)

Two things stood out from my impromptu, lengthy, and challenging conversation with Adam. First was his own story of growing up in the context of the church and not seeing authentic, biblical Christianity lived out in front of him. He consistently mentioned how he rarely (if ever) saw any wonder or amazement in the lives of the Christians he was around. Second, Adam said that he never saw God "show up" in a significant way, and never witnessed what he would affirm as an act of the supernatural.

> God's church is miraculous because it's *his* activity.

Adam and I talked at length about the miracles of Jesus detailed in the New Testament. He wasn't impressed. Adam said, "I would believe in Jesus if you could show me something supernatural. Something truly miraculous. I just don't see it." I paused, gathered my thoughts, and then answered Adam with the most visible, tangible, and miraculous thing I know of—God's church.[5] The foundation, construction, and expansion of God's church throughout human history is solidly within the framework of what theologians call a miracle—a less common kind of God's activity in which he arouses people's awe and wonder and bears witness to himself.[6]

God's church is miraculous because it's *his* activity. It's a group of people in awe of *his* grace and forgiveness. The church bears witness to *him*.

God's church, complete with scars and bruises of its own doing and from the constant angst-filled commentary leveled against it, continues to be the miraculous work of God. Rick McKinley writes, "When I think of the church I think miracle. Sometimes a funky, backwards, stubborn, and sinful miracle, but miracle nonetheless."[7]

Only God could take a group of twelve misfits from all walks of first-century life and develop it into a worldwide experience and expression of grace and truth. Only God could overcome the seemingly disastrous death of the group's leader, Jesus. Only God could raise Jesus from the dead. Only God could give Jesus the church as his current and one day fully redeemed, restored, and finished bride. God is at work building his church. "I will build my church, and the gates of hell shall not prevail against it" (Matt. 16:18).

This is not some meek and mild statement made by a man who doesn't understand fierce opposition. No. Jesus, the one who will soon after saying these words surrender to death on a cross at the hands of his opposition, confidently declares that he will build his church. He's responsible. He'll do the heavy lifting. And he will handle both the construction and the finishing work. But Jesus doesn't stop there. He then offers a promise of supreme confidence in his building prowess. Jesus says, *"and the gates of hell shall not prevail against it."*

Bottom line: Satan loses. Jesus and his people win.

All hell will break loose in an attempt to overcome and destroy God's church, but the demonic barrage will not be successful. Jesus has taken the action of creating and building his church, but he is also sustaining and protecting us as well. He will provide the power to stand firm against the threats, attacks, and all-out assaults on his church. Bruce Ware captures the power of Jesus's statement: "Satan and all of his demons simply cannot keep Christ from building his church exactly as he has planned and decided."[8]

But Jesus's plan is actually far different from what you or I might have chosen. It has been from the beginning. Consider, for a moment, the one person in the New Testament narrative you and I would probably *not* select as our representative. Do you have a guy in mind? The guy I'm thinking of can be argumentative, he's often irrational, and he seems to crack under pressure. Who's this anti-choice?

Peter.

Yet, of all the disciples God could have used as the representative of his church—that's exactly the one he chose—Peter! The same individual who lacked faith (Matt. 14:28–31), who denied Jesus in the weakest of ways (Matt. 26:31–35, 69–75), and whom Jesus himself referred to as "a stumbling block" (Matt. 16:23, NIV, ESV footnote).

Peter, this broken and redeemed work-in-progress is the same man who boldly proclaims of Jesus, "You are the Christ, the Son of the living God" (Matt. 16:16). Of all the disciples, God chose to reveal this truth to Peter. God chose the most unrefined, unfinished disciple to represent the confession of faith of all believers who would follow. Peter is the guy who becomes the believing, confessing, representative of all who profess Christ as Lord.

The irony of God's choice of Peter as our representative should not go unnoticed or under-appreciated, because most Christ followers that I know live lives a whole lot like Peter. We all have moments when we are boastful instead of humble, and we are faithless instead of faithful. We all have moments of righteous indignation when our rightness seems to be our real concern.

Bonhoeffer didn't miss the irony. He once wrote, "We all are Peter; . . . all of us, who simply live from our confession of faith in Christ, as the timid, faithless, fainthearted, and yet who live as people sustained by God."[9]

We all are Peter!

Yet Peter was God's choice to represent all who would follow Christ and ultimately become part of God's church. This reality should cause us to laugh at God's sense of humor. It should cause us to cry at God's grace for you and me. And it should cause our hearts to burst open and overflow with grace for our brothers and sisters in the faith.

We are a broken and redeemed work-in-progress, just like our brother Peter before us.

GOD'S VICTORIOUS COMMUNITY

The church is ultimately victorious; Jesus said it would be. But what does victory look like for God's church? Does it look like God's people being encouraged by the best Bible-based, Christ-centered teaching you've ever heard? Perhaps. Does it look like a gathering of God's people passionately singing the most God-honoring worship set you've ever experienced? Perhaps. Does it look like the most loved-on, well-fed, cleaned-up, and served gathering of people in need that you've ever seen? Perhaps. Or is God's ultimate vision for the church something completely different from what you and I might expect? I believe that it just might be a whole lot like what you and I are experiencing today.

I began this book by taking you to the pink-sand shores of the island of Bermuda, and specifically to an architectural structure that has long captured my attention and my imagination. Let's bring our journey full circle and return to the Unfinished Church that stands near one end of the island of Bermuda. Recall the grey nineteenth-century Gothic architectural structure. Recall the brokenness of the church building that lacks brilliantly colored stained-glass windows, sturdy wooden support beams, and beautifully crafted mosaic-tiled ceilings. Recall the timeless strength and imposing majesty of this structure even in its unfinished state.

Just as you've captured this image in your mind's eye—stay there. Do you sense the grandeur, the brokenness, the strength, the failures, the hope, the disappointments, and the potential? All are visible. All are palpable. All are real. To some, these things make the structure ugly. They make it something to be ignored, left behind, forgotten. To others, this condition gives it a mystery unlike anything else they've seen. The unique combination of brokenness and beauty is something to cherish and behold. This is God's church.

> The unique combination of brokenness and beauty is something to cherish and behold. This is God's church.

We have grandeur because God has called us his own. We have strength because we have been, and continue to be, redeemed. We also disappoint and fail our brothers and sisters in Christ—and those outside the faith—because we are broken. Most important of all is the hope that we have as God's people. Because Jesus is building his church, our potential is limitless!

God's called-out and redeemed community known as his church has a lot of faith yet to live out and to express. It happens as we accept and welcome those who look, think, and live out their faith differently than we do. It happens when we love one another, even when it's hard and we don't do it very well. It happens when we encourage one another, even when words of God-centered affirmation don't come naturally to us. It happens when we choose to serve one another, even when the work is dirty and difficult and comes with a cost. And it happens when we intentionally pursue unity with all of Christ's followers—because that's what Jesus desires for his people.

As each one of us faithfully submits to the Spirit to guide us and lead us, God is doing the refining work of sanctification in the lives of his followers. This leads us to welcome and love and encourage and serve and strive. And as we do, God continues to build his church through you and me. It's a church that is now flawed and imperfect, but will one day be made perfect and presented to Jesus as his beautiful, radiant, stunning, spotless bride. What is now an unfinished church, God's redeemed and broken work-in-progress, will one day become the finished church.

Church History

The truths discussed in this chapter have deep roots in the history of God's church. Consider the following example as you engage with these truths.

THE CANONS OF DORT

> *Christ's Death and Human Redemption Through It—Article 9: The Fulfillment of God's Plan*
>
> This plan, arising out of God's eternal love for his chosen ones, from the beginning of the world to the present time has been powerfully carried out and will also be carried out in the future, the gates of hell seeking vainly to prevail against it. As a result, the chosen are gathered into one, all in their own time, and there is always a church of believers founded on Christ's blood, a church which steadfastly loves, persistently worships, and—here and in all eternity—praises him as her Savior who laid down his life for her on the cross, as a bridegroom for his bride.[10]

Music

The themes discussed in this chapter have been expressed in both traditional and contemporary music. Below are a few titles to encourage you as you reflect on these themes.

> "Savior, Blessed Savior, Listen While We Sing," by Godfrey Thring
> "Wait and See," by Brandon Heath
> "Build Your Kingdom Here," by Rend Collective Experiment

Questions for Discussion

These questions have been developed for you to consider personally, answer honestly, and discuss openly—engaging your head and your heart—as you process the truths of this chapter together in community.

1. What is the first word or phrase that comes to your mind when you read the word *sanctification*? Explain.

2. Consider your own process of sanctification. In what area of your life is God currently at work sanding off the rough spots? Explain with details.

3. The importance of personal sanctification in the life of every Christ follower was a primary theme of this chapter. Discuss why this is so important.

4. Consider the idea that God's church is miraculous. Do you agree? If so, explain why. If not, explain why not.

5. Consider what you know about the life of the apostle Peter—passionate, irrational, and so on. Then read Matthew 16:13–19. What does this interaction show us about Peter? About Jesus? About Christians who follow in Peter's confession?

6. In Matthew's Gospel, Jesus says, "I will build my church, and the gates of hell shall not prevail against it." Describe how this shapes your view of God's church? Explain.

Notes

Chapter 1. God's Called-Out Community

1. Let me suggest reading 1 Pet. 2:9–10 over and over and over again until you begin to truly grasp the magnitude and depth of this biblical reality.
2. Jean Vanier, *Community and Growth* (New York: Paulist, 1989), 10.
3. Dietrich Bonhoeffer, *The Cost of Discipleship* (New York: Macmillan, 1963), 99.
4. Vern S. Poythress, *The Shadow of Christ in the Law of Moses* (Phillipsburg, NJ: P&R, 1991), 56.
5. Bruce Waltke, *An Old Testament Theology: An Exegetical, Canonical, and Thematic Approach* (Grand Rapids: Zondervan, 2007), 356.
6. Edmund P. Clowney, *The Message of 1 Peter: The Way of the Cross* (Downers Grove, IL: InterVarsity, 1988), 32–33.
7. Ibid., 34.
8. The pattern begins in Exodus 32 with Moses and a golden calf, but this lack of faithfulness continues throughout the Old Testament. Read the popular stories from Numbers, Judges, 1 and 2 Samuel, and 1 and 2 Kings, and you'll see that the history of God's people is sketchy at best when it comes to our faithfulness to God.
9. John R. W. Stott, *The Living Church: Convictions of a Lifelong Pastor* (Downers Grove, IL: InterVarsity, 2007), 52.
10. Christopher J. H. Wright, *The Mission of God: Unlocking the Bible's Grand Narrative* (Downers Grove, IL: InterVarsity, 2007), 6.
11. Quoted in Philip Schaff, *The Creeds of Christendom*, vol. 3, *The Evangelical Protestant Creeds* (Grand Rapids: Baker, 1984), 366–67.

Chapter 2. God's Redeemed Community

1. "For all have sinned and fall short of the glory of God" (Rom. 3:23).
2. Jerry Bridges, *The Gospel for Real Life: Turn to the Liberating Power of the Cross . . . Every Day* (Colorado Springs: NavPress, 2003), 79.
3. You'll find details of this Bermuda landmark in the introduction.
4. "Redeem, Redemption," in *Dictionary of Biblical Imagery*, ed. Leland

Ryken, James C. Wilhoit, and Tremper Longman III (Downers Grove, IL: InterVarsity, 1998), 698.

5. John R. W. Stott, *The Message of Romans: God's Good News for the World* (Downers Grove, IL: InterVarsity, 1994), 118.

6. F. F. Bruce, *Paul: Apostle of the Heart Set Free* (Grand Rapids: Eerdmans, 2000), 328.

7. David Platt, *Radical Together: Unleashing the People of God for the Purpose of God* (Colorado Springs: Multnomah, 2011), 31.

8. John R. W. Stott, *The Message of Galatians: Only One Way* (Downers Grove, IL: InterVarsity, 1968), 101.

9. The "are being" part of redemption is what's so hard for us to grasp. Because our current place of residence is a fallen, sin-filled world, we will continue to struggle with temptation and sin. While it may seem a bit cliché, this is why we are in need of God's redeeming work each day—in the here and now, not just for our ultimate redemption.

10. Oswald Chambers, "Redemption," in *The Complete Works of Oswald Chambers* (Grand Rapids: Discovery House, 2000), 557.

11. Quoted in *NIV Spirit of the Reformation Study Bible* (Grand Rapids: Zondervan, 2003), 2149.

Chapter 3. God's Eclectic, Intriguing, and Quirky Construction Crew

1. You know you're going to be there awhile, so you might as well look around and observe the diversity of God's creation.

2. The 1971 advertisement with teenagers from across the globe made the song "I'd Like to Teach the World to Sing (in Perfect Harmony)" such a part of our culture that many Coca-Cola-drinking adults can still sing it today some forty years later.

3. A pastor friend of mine once told me that he could look out over his congregation of three hundred on a Sunday morning and see the dividing lines of homeschool, Christian school, and public/charter school families in the seating patterns at the worship service.

4. Anne Lamott, *Bird by Bird: Some Instructions on Writing and Life* (New York: Anchor, 1994), 22.

5. Eugene Peterson, *A Long Obedience in the Same Direction: Discipleship in an Instant Society* (Downers Grove, IL: InterVarsity, 2000), 176.

6. John Ortberg, *Everybody's Normal Till You Get to Know Them* (Grand Rapids: Zondervan, 2003), 18.

7. Rick McKinley, *A Kingdom Called Desire: Confronted by the Love of a Risen King* (Grand Rapids: Zondervan, 2011), 139.

8. Matt Chandler, Josh Patterson, and Eric Geiger, *Creature of the Word: The Jesus-Centered Church* (Nashville, TN: B&H, 2012), 50.

9. Go for a fifteen-minute drive around town and pay special attention to the number of church denominations you see. You get the idea.

10. McKinley, *The Kingdom Called Desire*, 121.

11. You'd think that journeying with the Savior on the dusty roads of the ancient Near East might give a guy less pretense? Clearly not.
12. David Platt, *Radical Together: Unleashing the People of God for the Purpose of God* (Colorado Springs: Multnomah, 2011), 129.
13. James 1:27.
14. Quoted in *NIV Spirit of the Reformation Study Bible* (Grand Rapids: Zondervan, 2003), 2192.
15. Ibid., 2193.
16. Ibid.

Chapter 4. Love One Another: It Really Is about Jesus
1. Nouwen, Henri J. M., *The Return of the Prodigal Son: A Story of Homecoming* (New York: Doubleday, 1992), 1939.
2. Obviously, there are rules and regulations that any organization—Christian or other—is required to follow. I get this, as I've worked in vocational Christian ministry environments for nearly twenty years. I just can't get beyond the fact that a Christian organization would handle a man's sin in a way that was so unloving, and completely unlike the compassionate heart of Jesus—the One they seek to proclaim.
3. Tertullian, *Apology*, trans. S. Thelwall, chap. 39, http://www.earlychristianwritings.com/text/tertullian01.html.
4. Gerald L. Sittser, *Love One Another: Becoming the Church Jesus Longs For* (Downers Grove, IL: InterVarsity, 2008), 17.
5. Francis Chan, *Crazy Love: Overwhelmed by a Relentless God* (Colorado Springs: Cook, 2008), 93, 94.
6. Compassion International is a strategic ministry partner of the church where I serve.
7. Phil Ryken, *Loving the Way Jesus Loves* (Wheaton, IL: Crossway, 2012), 23–24.
8. David G. Benner, *Sacred Companions: The Gift of Spiritual Friendships and Direction* (Downers Grove, IL: InterVarsity, 2002), 34.
9. Quoted in *The Ecclesiastical History of Sozomen*, 5.16, in vol. 2 of *A Select Library of Nicene and Post-Nicene Fathers*, Series 2, ed. Philip Schaff and Henry Wace (New York: Christian Literature, 1890), 338.

Chapter 5. Encourage One Another: Giving a Blast of Gospel-Centered Truth
1. Research for this chapter comes from an updated version of the John Bunyan classic, *The New Pilgrim's Progress* (Grand Rapids: Discovery House, 1989).
2. At this point in Paul's life, he was still referred to as Saul in the biblical text. I'm choosing to make the name transition here for clarity and consistency.
3. "According to Luke, it was Barnabas whose good offices brought Paul and

the leaders of the Jerusalem church together. Although Paul says nothing of this, it is antecedently probable that someone acted as mediator, and all that we know of Barnabas suggests that he was the very man to act in this way. . . . His interposition on Paul's behalf in Jerusalem is completely in character." F. F. Bruce, *Paul: Apostle of the Heart Set Free* (Grand Rapids: Eerdmans, 2000), 83.

4. Paul's letters, from Romans through Philemon, constitute much of the New Testament.

5. Barnabas's ministry of encouragement has made such a lasting impact in the history of the church that his name is now synonymous with pastoral care and support ministry in the life of local churches everywhere.

6. Bruce, *Paul: Apostle of the Heart Set Free*, suggests that Paul's similar purpose and content for the Ephesians and the Colossians was based upon their being Gentile Christians who needed to be shown what was involved in their recent commitment to the way of Christ.

7. Typically, I try to avoid drawing attention to the root word, or the semantic field, of the original Greek. But the multiple meanings and uses of this one word are too significant to ignore.

8. Gerald L. Sittser, *Love One Another: Becoming the Church Jesus Longs For* (Downers Grove, IL: InterVarsity, 2008), 106–7.

9. Marva J. Dawn, *Truly the Community: Romans 12 and How to Be the Church* (Grand Rapids: Eerdmans, 1997), 124.

10. I know it's hard to believe in our tech-savvy culture, but some people still take the time to write handwritten notes. I actually received such a note this week. Fittingly, it had the words "Barnabas Note" printed on the front.

11. Kevin DeYoung, "Encourage One Another," Ligonier Ministries, the teaching fellowship of R.C. Sproul, http://www.ligonier.org/learn/articles/encourage-one-another/.

12. David G. Benner, *Sacred Companions: The Gift of Spiritual Friendship and Direction* (Downers Grove, IL: InterVarsity, 2002), 57.

13. Bunyan, *The New Pilgrim's Progress*, 35.

14. Ibid., 42.

15. See the introduction regarding the time (my wife) Bonnie and I served in Bermuda.

16. Sittser, *Love One Another*, 106.

17. Dietrich Bonhoeffer, *Life Together* (San Francisco: Harper & Row, 1954), 23.

18. Herman J. Selderhuis, *John Calvin: A Pilgrim's Life* (Downers Grove, IL: IVP Academic, 2009), 86–87. Research for this section came from Selderhuis's excellent book.

Chapter 6. Serve One Another: Putting Our Hands into Action—and More

1. Leonore Siegele-Wenschkewitz, "Christians against Nazis: The German Confessing Church," January 1, 1986, http://www.christianitytoday.com/ch/1986/issue9/9100.html.

2. Eric Metaxas, *Bonhoeffer: Pastor, Martyr, Prophet, Spy* (Nashville, TN: Thomas Nelson, 2010), 321.

3. Research on the life of Dietrich Bonhoeffer comes from ibid. and Edwin Robertson, *The Shame and the Sacrifice: The Life and Martyrdom of Dietrich Bonhoeffer* (New York: Macmillan, 1988).

4. Matt Chandler, Josh Patterson, and Eric Geiger, *Creature of the Word: The Jesus-Centered Church* (Nashville, TN: B&H, 2012), 66.

5. Gerald L. Sittser, *Love One Another: Becoming the Church Jesus Longs For* (Downers Grove, IL: InterVarsity, 2008), 92.

6. George Hobica, "The Things They Don't Tell You in the Safety Demo," January 29, 2013, http://www.airfarewatchdog.com/blog/13832148/the -things-they-dont-tell-you-in-the-safety-demo/.

7. One woman on our team actually committed to assisting her sponsored child go to college in Haiti!

8. Sittser, *Love One Another*, 96.

9. Rick McKinley, *A Kingdom Called Desire: Confronted by the Love of a Risen King* (Grand Rapids: Zondervan, 2011), 128.

10. There are numerous gifts listed in Scripture (Rom. 12:6–8; 1 Cor. 12:8–10; Eph. 4:11). Do you know how God has gifted you? If not, it's time to find out! Our church uses a book by Erik Rees, *S.H.A.P.E.: Finding and Fulfilling Your Unique Purpose for Life* (Grand Rapids: Zondervan, 2006). There are also many spiritual-gift assessments available online, including www .SpiritualGiftsTest.com.

11. David Augsburger, *Dissident Discipleship: A Spirituality of Self-Surrender, Love of God, and Love of Neighbor* (Grand Rapids: Brazos, 2006), 163.

12. John Stott, *The Living Church: Convictions of a Lifelong Pastor* (Downers Grove, IL: InterVarsity, 2007), 168–69, reformatted.

13. Quoted in *NIV Spirit of the Reformation Study Bible* (Grand Rapids: Zondervan, 2003), 2186.

Chapter 7. Dwell in Unity: Jesus Loves His Church, So You Should Too

1. Despite what you might assume from the title (it came from a bumper sticker) of Merchant's film, Dan loves Jesus and he loves God's people. He's committed to encouraging believers to love well and to foster unity within the church. The ultimate goal of his film was to overcome the culture wars that divide believers and unbelievers, and create an environment of honest, open dialogue. When I asked Dan his thoughts on what he learned about unity among God's people as he traveled the country making his film, he said, "It is difficult to learn from each other and share with each other when we are divided. Conversely, I've seen some remarkable, moving, encouraging, surprising things occur when some version of unity happens. . . . I suspect the Holy Spirit shows up in that space created when we find reasons to be together instead of separate."

2. Sadly, this is likely because they had never received so much as a hint of grace or forgiveness from other believers themselves.

3. David Kinnaman and Gabe Lyons coauthored a book *Unchristian: What a New Generation Really Thinks about Christianity . . . and Why It Matters* (Grand Rapids: Baker, 2007), presenting their research about the unfavorable view that "outsiders" have of Christians, and the increasing percentage of sixteen- to twenty-nine-year-olds who are leaving the church.

4. The most honest, well-articulated book is written by Michael Spencer, a.k.a. The Internet Monk, titled *Mere Churchianity* (Colorado Springs: WaterBrook, 2010).

5. The most recent article was Andrew Sullivan's April 9, 2012, cover story for the Easter edition of *Newsweek* magazine titled, *Forget the Church, Follow Jesus.*

6. Eugene Peterson, *Practice Resurrection: A Conversation on Growing Up in Christ* (Grand Rapids: Eerdmans, 2010), 176.

7. Just consider for a moment a pair of prominent brotherly relationships in the Old Testament: Cain and Abel, and Joseph and his many brothers.

8. Eugene Peterson, *A Long Obedience in the Same Direction: Discipleship in an Instant Society* (Downers Grove, IL: InterVarsity, 2000), 181.

9. Mark Ross, "In Essentials Unity, in Non-Essentials Liberty, in All Things Charity," Ligonier Ministries, the teaching fellowship of R.C. Sproul, September 16, 2009, http://www.ligonier.org/learn/articles/essentials-unity -non-essentials-liberty-all-things/.

10. Philip Schaff, *History of the Christian Church*, vol. 6, *Modern Christianity: The German Reformation*, 2nd ed. (New York: Charles Scribner's Sons, 1916), 650.

11. Mark Buchanan, *Your Church Is Too Safe: Why Following Christ Turns the World Upside-Down* (Grand Rapids: Zondervan, 2011), 171.

12. Jesse Rice, *The Church of Facebook: How the Hyperconnected Are Redefining Community* (Colorado Springs: Cook, 2009), 179.

13. On one of the nights that I was writing this chapter, I was putting my daughter Bethany to bed when she gave me a big hug and said, "Daddy, I like you *and* I love you!" I couldn't help but smile and consider how our heavenly Father would feel if we could say the same about his church.

14. Steve Brown, "Church 'R' Us," Key Life Network radio broadcast, February 25, 2008.

15. Kevin DeYoung, epilogue to DeYoung and Ted Kluck, *Why We Love the Church: In Praise of Institutions and Organized Religion* (Chicago: Moody, 2009), 211–12.

16. Marva J. Dawn, *Truly the Community: Romans 12 and How to Be the Church* (Grand Rapids: Eerdmans, 1992), 245.

17. Charles W. Colson, *The Faith: Given Once, for All* (Grand Rapids: Zondervan, 2008), 155.

Chapter 8. Jesus Finishes His Building Project

1. Rom. 6:22; 2 Cor. 3:18; and 1 Thess. 5:23–24 are just a few helpful verses on sanctification.

2. Owen Strachan, "Sanctification: Being Authentically Messed Up Is Not Enough," in *Don't Call It a Comeback: The Old Faith for a New Day*, ed. Kevin DeYoung (Wheaton, IL: Crossway, 2011), 108.

3. J. I. Packer, *Concise Theology: A Guide to Historic Christian Beliefs* (Wheaton, IL: Foundation for Reformation, 1993), 170–71.

4. Kevin DeYoung, "The Glory of Plodding," *Tabletalk*, May 1, 2010, http://www.ligonier.org/learn/articles/glory-plodding/.

5. Certainly the foundation, growth, and expansion of God's church does not fit within the framework of those who would define it as a work contrary to the laws of God or contrary to God's natural law. What their definition offers in science, it lacks in view of God's providence.

6. This research is from Wayne Grudem's excellent reference book *Systematic Theology: An Introduction to Biblical Doctrine* (Grand Rapids: Zondervan, 1994), chap. 52.

7. Rick McKinley, *A Kingdom Called Desire: Confronted by the Love of a Risen King* (Grand Rapids: Zondervan, 2011), 135.

8. Bruce Ware, *Big Truths for Young Hearts: Teaching and Learning the Greatness of God* (Wheaton, IL: Crossway, 2009), 192.

9. Dietrich Bonhoeffer, *A Testament to Freedom: The Essential Writings of Dietrich Bonhoeffer*, ed. Geffrey B. Kelly and F. Burton Nelson (San Francisco: HarperCollins, 1995), 215.

10. Quoted in *NIV Spirit of the Reformation Study Bible* (Grand Rapids: Zondervan, 2003), 2166.

General Index

Abraham, 42, 48–49
Augsburger, David, 122

Benner, David, 89, 100
Bonhoeffer, Dietrich, 21, 26, 106, 110–13, 156
Bridges, Jerry, 40
brokenness, 15, 43, 53, 157
Brown, Steve, 136–37
Bruce, F. F., 46–47, 163–64
Bucer, Martin, 107–8
Buchanan, Mark, 133–34
Buechner, Frederick, 75
Bunyan, John, 92–93, 100

calling, 22–27, 103
Calvin, John, 107–8
Canons of Dort, 158
Chambers, Oswald, 38, 53
Chan, Francis, 86
Chandler, Matt, 68, 110, 114–15
Christian maturity, 97
church
    as a called-out community, 28–33, 157–58
    disunity in, 126–29
    diversity in, 65–67, 147
    division within, 68–71
    and encouraging one another, 92–106, 150
    and loving one another, 82–89
    as a redeemed community, 53–54
    seeking unity within, 134–40, 147
    as a serving community, 113–24
church denominations, 132
church history, 36, 54–55, 72–73, 89–90, 106–7, 124, 140–41, 158
Clowney, Edmund, 32
Colson, Chuck, 139
covenant faithfulness, 28–29
culture wars, 165

Dawn, Marva, 98, 139
DeYoung, Kevin, 99, 126, 137, 152

election, 29–33
eternal life, 44, 46
exodus, 42–43

faith, 46, 48–49, 101
faith journey, 51, 82, 84, 93–95, 100–104, 147–50
forgiveness, 41, 54, 68, 138–39, 154
freedom, 115
French Confession of Faith, 36

Geiger, Eric, 68, 110, 114–15
Gnosticism, 140
God
    glory of, 26
    honoring of, 47
    image of, 62–63
    love of, 77–82
    presence of, 131

Scripture Index